DON'T OPEN THE BOX

A beginner's guide to quantum computing

Tommy Wassgren

AF677450

While every precaution has been taken in the preparation of this book, the publisher assumes no responsibility for errors or omissions, or for damages resulting from the use of the information contained herein.

DON'T OPEN THE BOX

First edition. August 14, 2025.

Copyright © 2025 Tommy Wassgren.

ISBN: 979-8231853052

Written by Tommy Wassgren.

Table of Contents

To the brilliant minds advancing quantum computing, turning science fiction into reality, one breakthrough at a time.

Introduction

What if we had a computer so powerful it could crack problems that today's most advanced supercomputers wouldn't finish in a lifetime? Imagine the Starship Enterprise from Star Trek, a system that instantly translates alien languages, maps entire galaxies in real-time, and makes split-second decisions with limitless intelligence. A machine that doesn't just calculate faster but thinks in ways we've never seen before. This isn't just science fiction, it's the future quantum computing could turn into reality.

Unlike the classical computers we know, quantum computers work on the principles of quantum mechanics, a field that redefined our understanding of the universe on the smallest scales. Developed nearly a century ago, quantum mechanics introduced concepts that challenge our usual sense of logic, like superposition, quantum entanglement, and wave-particle duality. Early pioneers like Albert Einstein, Niels Bohr, Erwin Schrödinger, and J. Robert Oppenheimer laid the foundations of this field, reshaping our view of reality. Schrödinger's famous thought experiment of a "cat" that is simultaneously alive and dead illustrates superposition, a principle at the core of quantum computing that defies our everyday experiences with technology.

Today, quantum mechanics reaches beyond textbooks and labs, it is part of popular culture, sparking curiosity and influencing new stories. Films like Oppenheimer, which follows Dr. J. Robert Oppenheimer's life and atomic research, examine the significant impact of scientific discovery. Shows like Devs picture quantum computers advanced enough to predict past and future events. These stories hint at the potential of quantum technology to alter our understanding of reality, decision-making, and human potential.

Quantum computing's impact could reach even further when paired with another groundbreaking technology, artificial intelligence. AI already powers data-driven insights in fields like healthcare, finance, and logistics. When combined with quantum computing, the potential of AI could expand dramatically, paving the way for breakthroughs in personalized medicine, climate science, materials engineering, and more. Together, quantum computing and AI open up possibilities we're only beginning to imagine, from more precise simulations to real-time optimization and smarter decision-making systems.

This book will take you through the world of quantum computing. We'll explore its origins, look at its current advancements, and consider what the future might hold. By the end, you'll understand how quantum mechanics and computing come together, why they could change the way we solve problems, and how this shift might influence the future of human knowledge.

This book is for anyone curious about quantum computing, whether you're just starting to learn about it or already have a passion for technology. It aims to explain the science, applications, and potential of quantum computing in an accessible way. Together, we'll explore a field that, while quite tricky to grasp, has the potential to change how we think, solve problems, and innovate in the 21st century.

About this book

The book is structured in four parts, each designed to deepen understanding step-by-step, balancing technical explanations with accessible language. Words included in the glossary (Appendix D: Glossary) are **bolded** the first time they appear, making it easier to identify and revisit key terms as needed. Additionally, *italicized words* and phrases are used to highlight important concepts throughout the text. Here's a brief guide to how the book unfolds:

- **Part I – Past and present:** This section covers the basics of quantum computing and its current state, explaining foundational concepts like superposition and quantum entanglement and tracing the historical contributions of figures like Oppenheimer.

- **Part II – Beyond today:** This part offers a glimpse of quantum's future impact across industries, highlighting both the exciting possibilities and the ethical considerations, including workforce implications and societal shifts.

- **Part III – Reflections:** Part three brings together the key insights and invites readers to think about how quantum technology could affect the world.

- **Part IV – Appendices:** The fourth and final section provides additional resources, from practical guides on quantum programming to a glossary and focused look at quantum machine learning (QML), allowing readers to explore further.

Preface

When I first began learning about quantum computing, it felt like stepping into the pages of science fiction. The concepts of qubits, superposition, and quantum entanglement were astonishing; not because they seemed almost unbelievable, but because they are real phenomena grounded in quantum mechanics. What amazed me even more was how researchers are applying these principles to build groundbreaking technologies, innovations that might change the world.

As someone who has always loved sci-fi, I found this both exciting and humbling. Quantum computing captures the same sense of wonder that drew me to those stories, but it's happening here and now thanks to the incredible work of scientists and engineers around the globe.

This book is my way of sharing that sense of discovery. Quantum computing can seem unfamiliar at first, but it's something anyone can appreciate with the right explanations. I've worked hard to make this book easy to follow while keeping the wonder alive.

For me, quantum computing feels like one of humanity's greatest ventures, a chance *to boldly go where no one* has gone before, exploring possibilities that once seemed like fiction. I hope this book inspires you to discover the excitement and potential of this extraordinary field. I hope this book sparks your curiosity and interest in the potential of this extraordinary field.

Disclaimer

The information provided in this book is for educational and informational purposes only. While every effort has been made to ensure the accuracy and reliability of the content, the author makes no guarantees regarding the completeness or applicability of the material to specific situations.

This book is not intended to serve as professional or technical advice. Readers are encouraged to consult experts or conduct further research for more in-depth information on quantum computing and related fields.

The author shall not be held liable for any errors, omissions, or outcomes arising from the use of the information in this book. Any opinions expressed are those of the author and do not represent the views of any organization or institution.

PAST AND PRESENT

Part I

A history of quantum discoveries

The development of **quantum computing** didn't start with computers, it began with a scientific revolution that changed our understanding of the universe. In the early 20th century, scientists observed strange behaviors in experiments that didn't follow Newton's laws, which had been the standard for understanding motion and interactions.

Newton's laws describe a predictable world: every action has an equal and opposite reaction, and objects remain at rest or in motion unless acted upon. But as scientists explored the atomic and subatomic levels, they discovered these rules didn't always apply on the smallest scales.

Experiments with light and particles revealed phenomena that seemed to defy classical expectations, hinting at a reality much more intricate and mysterious than once imagined. This led to the birth of **quantum mechanics**, a field that introduced a new set of principles for understanding matter and energy at the smallest scales. This chapter examines the key discoveries and ideas that laid the foundation for quantum computing, showing how historic breakthroughs in quantum mechanics opened the door to realizing the remarkable potential of quantum technology.

The birth of quantum theory

To understand quantum computing, it's helpful to distinguish three related terms: quantum mechanics, **quantum physics**, and quantum computing.

Quantum mechanics is the study of particle behavior on the smallest scales, such as atoms and subatomic particles. It explains phenomena that seem unusual by classical standards, like particles existing in multiple states at once (**superposition**) or being "linked" across distances (**quantum entanglement**).

Quantum physics, often used interchangeably with quantum mechanics, more broadly covers the study of these behaviors and their applications throughout different fields, including chemistry, materials science, and biology.

Quantum computing applies principles of quantum mechanics to computation. It relies on **qubits**, which unlike **classical bits** can exist in multiple states simultaneously, enabling certain problems to be solved much faster than with traditional computers.

These distinctions clarify how each concept fits together: quantum mechanics provides the foundational principles, quantum physics explores their applications, and quantum computing uses these ideas to advance technology.

The double-slit experiment

One of the most famous experiments in quantum physics is the **double-slit experiment**, which reveals the strange and fascinating behavior of light and particles. Think of shining a flashlight through a single narrow opening, or slit, cut into a piece of cardboard, onto a screen behind it. A slit is simply a small gap that allows light to pass through. On the screen, you'll see a single stripe of light directly behind the slit, the result you'd expect if light travels in straight lines like tiny particles.

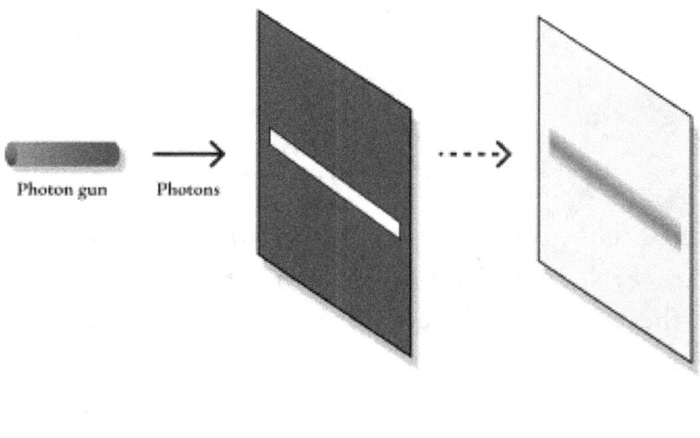

Single slit – one bright stripe

Now, let's add another slit parallel to the first one. Instead of seeing two stripes of light on the screen, something remarkable happens: the light creates a pattern of bright and dark stripes, called an **interference** pattern. This kind of pattern is exactly what you'd expect if light were behaving like a wave, spreading out through both slits and overlapping.

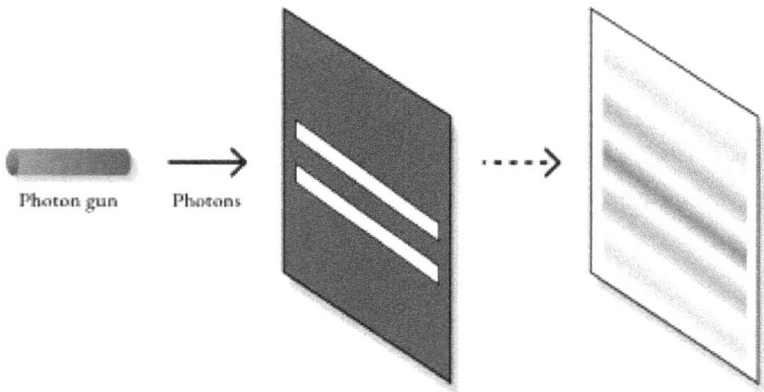

Double slit – wave pattern appears

It's similar to the ripples in a pond when you drop two stones close together. Each stone creates circular waves that spread outward across the surface. As these waves move, they eventually overlap. In some places, the ripples combine to create larger waves. This is called constructive interference. In other places, the ripples cancel each other out, creating flat areas which is called destructive interference. The bright and dark stripes on the screen in the double-slit experiment mimic this pattern, showing that the light behaves like overlapping waves as it passes through the two slits.

Then scientists took it a step further. Instead of shining a continuous beam of light, they sent individual particles of light, called **photons**, through the slits one at a time. Surprisingly, even when the photons were sent individually, the interference pattern still appeared on the screen. It was as though each photon acted like a wave, somehow passing through both slits at once and interfering with itself.

The genuine mystery began when scientists tried to observe the photons directly. By placing detectors near the slits to see which slit each photon passed through, the interference pattern disappeared. Instead of behaving like waves, the photons acted like particles, creating two distinct lines on the screen, one behind each slit. It was as if the act of observing the photons changed their behavior.

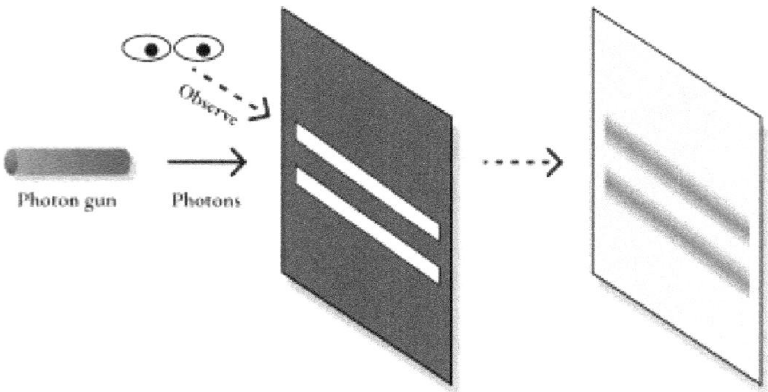

Double slit with observation – two distinct stripes

This puzzling phenomenon, known as **wave-particle duality**, demonstrated that particles like photons (and, as later experiments showed, **electrons** and other particles) can behave as both waves and particles. Their behavior depends on whether they are being observed. It almost sounds like magic, doesn't it? Wave-particle duality overturned classical ideas about particles always having a definite position or path, introducing a key idea in quantum mechanics: *the act of measurement itself can influence the outcome.*

The Heisenberg principle: Uncertainty and pop culture

One of the most intriguing ideas in quantum mechanics is **Heisenberg's Uncertainty Principle**. At its core, it says that you can't precisely know both the position and velocity of a particle at the same time. For example, if you know exactly where a particle is, you can't know how fast it's moving. And if you know how fast it's moving, its exact location becomes uncertain. This isn't because of a flaw in our measuring tools, it's a fundamental property of the quantum world.

The principle is named after Werner Heisenberg, a German physicist who was one of the founders of quantum mechanics. In 1927, Heisenberg proposed the uncertainty principle as part of his groundbreaking work to explain the behavior of particles at atomic and subatomic scales. His insights helped redefine physics, shifting it away from the predictability of classical mechanics and introducing the idea that the very act of observation affects reality. For his contributions, Heisenberg was awarded the Nobel Prize in Physics in 1932.

To make this more relatable, picture trying to catch a fast-moving fly in a dark room. If you shine a flashlight on the fly to see where it is, the light might disturb it, causing it to change direction or speed. In the quantum world, something similar happens when you try to measure a particle. The very act of *observing the particle changes its behavior*, making it impossible to pin down both its position and velocity with absolute precision.

Heisenberg's principle has even found its way into pop culture. In the TV show Breaking Bad, the main character, Walter White, adopts the alias "Heisenberg". On the surface, it's a nod to his background as a chemistry teacher. But it also reflects the unpredictable and chaotic nature of his double life as a drug producer. Like the uncertainty in quantum particles, Walter's actions set off a chain of events with far-reaching and unpredictable consequences, making the alias a fitting metaphor.

This principle changed how we think about reality. In the classical world, objects like a car or a baseball have predictable paths and speeds. But in the quantum world, particles don't have fixed positions or velocities until they are observed, introducing a new way of understanding nature on the smallest scales.

Enter Schrödinger's cat, superposition, and the coin flip

The 1935 thought experiment introduced by physicist **Erwin Schrödinger** is a famous illustration of quantum principles, particularly superposition. In his experiment, Schrödinger imagined a sealed box containing a cat (hence **Schrödinger's cat**), a vial of poison, and a radioactive atom. The atom has an equal chance of decaying or remaining stable, which is connected to a mechanism that, if triggered, will break the vial and release the poison, killing the cat. Until the box is opened, and the atom's state is observed, the cat could be *both alive and dead at the same time.*

Schrödinger didn't suggest that an actual cat would exist in both states, but he used this paradox to highlight a unique feature of quantum mechanics: particles can exist in multiple states simultaneously. This idea is known as superposition, which is essential to quantum computing. In quantum mechanics, a particle like an electron or a photon can be in a superposition of states, much like Schrödinger's hypothetical cat.

To understand superposition in quantum computing, envision a coin flip. In classical computing, a classical bit (like a coin) is 0 or 1 (heads or tails) once it lands. Each classical bit has a fixed state that powers standard computing tasks. But in quantum computing, a qubit (quantum bit) is like a coin spinning in the air, existing in a superposition of both heads and tails, or 0 and 1, until it *collapses* to one state when measured. This unique ability of qubits to represent multiple states at once gives quantum computers the power to explore *many possibilities simultaneously*, opening doors to calculations that are not possible for classical computers.

The atomic age and Oppenheimer's influence

As quantum mechanics progressed, it opened the door to atomic research that changed history. During World War II, **J. Robert Oppenheimer,** known as the *father of the atomic bomb*, led the Manhattan Project, which brought together top physicists to develop nuclear weapons. This work helped establish atomic and particle physics, both of which still connect with quantum research today. Oppenheimer's role showed both the power and the risks of scientific progress, a tension that remains relevant in today's discussions about quantum computing.

At the Institute for Advanced Study in Princeton, Oppenheimer worked alongside **Albert Einstein**. While Einstein's theories laid the groundwork for modern physics, he questioned whether quantum mechanics told the full story. Oppenheimer embraced it. Their views differed, but both were deeply committed to science.

Oppenheimer was more than a physicist. He had a strong interest in literature, philosophy, and languages. His ethical concerns about the bomb were captured in his well-known quote, "Now I am become Death, the destroyer of worlds," taken from the Hindu scripture *Bhagavad Gita*. This reflection plays a central role in the 2023 film *Oppenheimer*, directed by Christopher Nolan and starring Cillian Murphy.

Later in life, Oppenheimer faced political backlash. During the Red Scare, he lost his security clearance over suspected ties to communism. Still, his reflections on knowledge and responsibility continue to shape how we think about science and its place in society.

After the war, both computing and quantum physics advanced quickly. Early computers were built to handle large calculations, while physicists explored atomic structure in more detail. These developments helped shape the quantum technology we are exploring today.

Quantum Multiverses and the Marvel Universe

Quantum mechanics has inspired some of the most imaginative storytelling in modern pop culture, especially in the Marvel Cinematic Universe (MCU). Movies like *Doctor Strange in the Multiverse of Madness* and *Ant-Man and the Wasp* take audiences into alternate realities and subatomic worlds, where heroes and villains experience phenomena reminiscent of quantum theory. Ant-Man's Quantum Realm, for example, is a world shaped by quantum mechanics, where scale and time behave unpredictably, and characters encounter multiple potential realities.

Marvel's multiverse concept also connects to ideas in quantum mechanics. While quantum physics doesn't prove parallel universes, interpretations like the **Many-worlds theory** suggest that every quantum event could lead to branching realities, creating *multiverses* where different versions of us exist based on different outcomes. In this way, Marvel's portrayal of a multiverse draws on genuine scientific theories, even if they remain speculative.

From theory to technology

Over the 20th century, quantum mechanics evolved from abstract theory into the basis for technologies we now use every day. This shift began when scientists found ways to apply quantum principles to real-world problems.

One early breakthrough was the invention of the laser in the 1960s. By controlling atomic energy states, researchers created concentrated beams of light with unique properties. Lasers quickly became essential in medicine, telecommunications, and manufacturing, now used in everything from barcode scanners to surgical tools.

Another major development was the **transistor**, invented in 1947. Transistors control electron flow using quantum principles and are the core of modern electronics. Without them, we wouldn't have computers, smartphones, or digital devices. Quantum mechanics made it possible to work with materials at the atomic level, allowing the creation of compact, efficient circuits.

Quantum theory also enabled advances in medical imaging. MRI machines use the behavior of atomic nuclei in magnetic fields to produce detailed internal images. This non-invasive method has transformed diagnostics and treatment across healthcare.

Atomic clocks are among the most precise timekeeping devices ever built, showing how quantum technology has practical impact. Unlike mechanical or quartz clocks, they measure time using the vibrations of atoms, usually cesium or rubidium. Cesium clocks, for example, define a second based on energy transitions within cesium atoms, achieving accuracy within one second over millions of years. These clocks are used to maintain Coordinated Universal Time (UTC), managed by institutions such as the **National Institute of Standards and Technology (NIST)** in the U.S. and the National Physical Laboratory (NPL) in the U.K. A global network of atomic clocks, linked through satellites and the internet, keeps time synchronized around the world.

Their precision is essential across many fields. GPS systems rely on atomic clocks to time signals from satellites, enabling accurate positioning. In telecommunications, they synchronize networks to support mobile communication and internet traffic. Financial systems use atomic timing to record transactions down to the microsecond, especially in high-frequency trading. In science, precise timing helps astronomers track celestial events, calculate orbits, and study gravitational waves.

A newer generation, optical atomic clocks, operates at higher frequencies using visible light. These could redefine timekeeping standards and support advances such as detecting gravitational shifts, improving navigation systems, and enhancing scientific measurement.

Quantum sensors show how quantum mechanics is shaping modern technology. Using superposition and entanglement, they achieve sensitivity beyond classical devices. These sensors are used in medical imaging, geological surveys, and navigation, detecting tiny changes in magnetic or gravitational fields. For example, quantum-enhanced MRI could one day produce ultra-high-resolution images to support early disease detection.

Classical vs. quantum computing

Before exploring how quantum computers work, it's useful to look at how classical computers handle information. This provides context for what makes quantum systems different and why qubits matter.

Understanding classical computing

Classical computing, which underpins all digital technology, operates with binary classical bits. By arranging these classical bits into sequences, classical computers perform calculations through logical operations, handling instructions in a step-by-step manner.

Think of each classical bit as a switch that's *on (1)* or *off (0)*. To carry out computations, classical computers link thousands or even millions of these classical bits, creating patterns of on/off states that represent data. This approach is effective for many tasks but encounters limits as calculations become increasingly complicated.

The power of exponential growth

Exponential growth is a phenomenon where quantities increase at a rapidly accelerating rate, often leading to unexpected and dramatic outcomes. This growth pattern is fundamental in fields like technology, biology, and finance. A classic way to illustrate exponential growth is the *folding paper* example.

Suppose we have a standard sheet of paper, roughly 0.1 millimeters thick. If you fold it in half once, it doubles to 0.2 millimeters; fold it again, and it's 0.4 millimeters thick. By the tenth fold, it has reached a thickness of about 10.24 centimeters; roughly the height of a stack of textbooks. But the real surprise comes as folding continues. By the 42nd fold, the paper's thickness would exceed the distance from Earth to the moon. Fold it just one more time, and the paper's thickness would span the distance from the Earth to the moon and back again! This example captures how exponential growth, while seemingly slow at first, quickly reaches extraordinary heights once momentum builds.

Moore's Law

Exponential growth in computing has been evident through **Moore's Law**, a concept introduced by Intel co-founder Gordon Moore. He observed that the number of transistors on a microchip *doubles approximately every two years*. Transistors, tiny semiconductor devices that act as electronic switches, are essential for modern computers. They control the flow of electricity, enabling circuits to process information in binary form (representing either a 0 or a 1). This ability forms the backbone of all computer functions, from running programs to storing data.

The consistent doubling of transistor counts has led to remarkable advances in computing power while simultaneously reducing costs. This steady growth has driven progress in various technologies, from computers to smartphones and beyond. Back in the 1970s, a computer chip might have held only a few thousand transistors, while today's high-end processors contain billions. This exponential growth in transistor density has pushed technology forward in ways that would have seemed unimaginable just a few decades ago. Much like folding a piece of paper that rapidly thickens with each fold, each leap in transistor density has driven remarkable changes, powering the digital revolution and making innovations like smartphones and advanced scientific simulations possible.

Exponential growth seems to be a recurring pattern in digital technology, not just in computing hardware, but across the systems that shape modern life. Mobile and cloud technologies have scaled dramatically over the past two decades, changing how people connect, work, and store data. Similarly, Artificial Intelligence (AI), particularly the development of **large language models (LLMs)**, has expanded at a fast pace, increasing in size and capability in a short amount of time.

The limits of classical computing

Moore's Law, however, is reaching its physical limits. While transistors have been shrinking steadily, they are now nearing atomic scales. At these tiny scales, quantum effects, such as tunneling (where particles pass through barriers they usually wouldn't), interfere with transistor function. It's like trying to write with a pencil sharpened to a needlepoint. The tip becomes too fragile to use effectively, making further refinement impractical. This means that continuing to boost computing power through traditional transistor miniaturization alone is becoming impractical.

These limitations are especially problematic for solving increasingly complex problems, like simulating chemical reactions or optimizing massive logistical networks. Such challenges *demand processing power beyond what classical computers, even at their peak, can offer.*

Classical vs. quantum parallel processing

Classical computers increase processing power by adding more cores, which allows them to handle multiple tasks simultaneously, a method known as parallel processing. Think of a task like assembling a puzzle; each core works on a distinct part, speeding up the process.

Yet, even with multiple cores, classical computers eventually hit a ceiling. Each core must still process tasks one at a time, and as more cores are added, the system requires more power. It's like trying to solve multiple puzzles on a single table. Eventually, space runs out.

Quantum computing, however, allows true **parallelism through qubits**, which can process multiple possibilities at once. Going back to the puzzle analogy, say that each puzzle piece could simultaneously try out multiple positions, almost instantly finding the correct spot. Quantum computers achieve this because each qubit can exist in multiple states at the same time, unlike classical bits limited to 0 or 1. This ability to test many solutions in parallel gives quantum computing its unique power, especially for tasks involving **optimization** and **quantum simulation**.

Fundamental principles of quantum mechanics

Quantum mechanics brings forward principles that depart entirely from the binary, step-by-step logic of classical computing allowing quantum computers to process information uniquely.

We've already looked at superposition (the idea that a qubit can exist in more than one state at the same time, as illustrated by Schrödinger's cat). That principle is one of several that make quantum computing work very differently from classical computing.

Another core idea is wave-particle duality, which shows that particles, such as electrons (tiny charged particles) and photons (light particles), can behave as *both* particles and waves. In contrast to our everyday experience (where something is distinctly one thing or another, like a rock or ripples in water) quantum mechanics allows these particles to interact in ways that resemble overlapping waves forming new patterns. This wave-particle duality enables quantum computers to manage information in ways that traditional computers cannot.

Quantum entanglement is another remarkable feature of quantum mechanics. Picture two mirrors in different rooms. If something changes in front of one, the other reflects it instantly. Similarly, entangled particles maintain a connection such that a change in one is immediately mirrored by the other, regardless of distance. This property enables entangled qubits in a quantum computer to coordinate calculations more effectively, as changes in one qubit instantly affect its entangled counterpart.

Interference, a concept familiar with wave behavior in water or sound, also plays a key role in quantum computing. Just as overlapping waves can reinforce or cancel each other out, quantum particles such as photons or electrons exhibit interference. Quantum computers exploit interference to adjust the probabilities of different outcomes, enhancing the likelihood of correct answers and reducing that of incorrect ones. This ability to "tune" outcomes makes quantum computers particularly efficient at solving complex problems.

These principles allow quantum computers to manage information in ways that classical computers cannot, unlocking new possibilities for dealing with challenges that were previously beyond reach.

The power of qubits

Picture a quantum computer as an extensive network of roads, each leading to a different solution. A qubit is like a car able to move across multiple roads at once, exploring several routes simultaneously. By representing both 0 and 1 at the same time, a qubit "drives" through immense amounts of information, achieving speeds and capacities that classical computers simply cannot match.

Qubits come in different forms, each designed with unique physical principles and suited to specific tasks. **Superconducting qubits**, for example, are based on superconducting circuits cooled to nearly absolute zero, where resistance disappears, allowing high stability. These qubits are known for their speed and are used in systems like **Google's Sycamore** and **IBM's Eagle**, known for advances in processing speed and reliability.

Trapped ion qubits, which involve charged atoms held by electromagnetic fields, are known for precision and can operate at higher temperatures than superconducting qubits, though they are typically slower. **IonQ** and **Honeywell** have implemented this technology in their systems, with IonQ's quantum computers already supporting research in fields like chemistry and materials science.

Photonic qubits use particles of light (photons) to transfer quantum information, making them ideal for communication. Because photons can travel long distances with little interference, photonic qubits are especially suited for data transmission. Canadian company **Xanadu** uses photonic qubits to explore broader applications in **quantum communication**.

Researchers are also developing specialized qubits for unique applications. **Spin qubits**, which rely on the spin of electrons or nuclei, are studied for integration with traditional silicon technology. **Quantum dot qubits**, which use tiny semiconductor particles to trap single electrons, show potential for scaling within silicon-based systems, with research led by the University of New South Wales. **Diamond (NV center) qubits**, using specific defects in diamonds, are effective at room temperature and are explored for quantum sensing. Quantum Diamond Technologies is actively developing these applications. Meanwhile, experimental **topological** and **Majorana qubits** seek to increase stability by creating highly resistant structures, an area of interest for Microsoft and Delft University.

Each qubit type has strengths and limitations, encouraging researchers to explore combinations to build reliable and scalable quantum systems.

However, qubits present significant challenges. Their delicate nature makes it difficult to maintain **coherence**, the period during which a qubit can hold its quantum state. Longer coherence times allow for more calculations, yet current coherence periods range only from microseconds to milliseconds. Extending coherence time requires highly controlled environments and specialized materials.

Another major challenge is **error rates**. Qubits are highly sensitive, and small environmental changes, from temperature shifts to electromagnetic noise, can disrupt them and cause computational errors. Researchers address this through **error-correcting** codes that use additional qubits to detect and correct mistakes. While effective, these techniques require more resources and advanced control systems.

Decoherence, or the loss of a qubit's quantum properties because of outside influences, complicates quantum computing further. Keeping qubits stable is like trying to keep an ice cube from melting on a warm day, it demands extremely low temperatures and strict environmental control. Materials and shielding techniques help qubits keep their quantum states despite external disturbances.

Scaling up quantum systems poses additional hurdles. With each added qubit, maintaining stability and control across the entire system becomes exponentially harder. Large systems often experience **quantum crosstalk**, where one qubit's behavior unintentionally affects its neighbors. Innovations in qubit design, cooling, and error correction are critical to developing quantum computers that can handle large, interconnected systems.

Overcoming these challenges is essential for realizing the full potential of quantum computing. Researchers are making progress in improving qubit stability, reliability, and scalability through exotic materials, novel architectures, and refined error correction techniques. Each step forward brings us closer to unlocking the true potential of quantum computing, with the capacity to reframe domains and handle elaborate challenges beyond the reach of classical technology.

Quantum computing's exponential potential

The idea of exponential growth is essential for picturing the future of quantum computing. Quantum systems can process information in different ways, using the properties of qubits (as previously explained) to explore an ever-widening range of possibilities. Each additional qubit doubles the number of states a quantum computer can represent, meaning a system with n qubits can hold 2^n possible states at once. This exponential increase in qubit power could open new doors throughout various fields.

In classical computing, each added classical bit only increases the system's power linearly, representing just one more state (either 0 or 1). Quantum computing, however, operates exponentially:

- **Single qubit:** Represents $2^1 = 2$ states simultaneously (0 and 1).
- **Two qubits:** Represents $2^2 = 4$ states at once (00, 01, 10, and 11).
- **Three qubits:** Expands to $2^3 = 8$ states, and so on.

With each new qubit, the number of states doubles, so a 10-qubit quantum system can represent all 1,024 possible states simultaneously, while a classical 10-bit system can only hold one of those states at a time. This exponential capacity allows quantum computers to explore multiple possibilities in parallel.

This growth resembles Moore's Law, where classical computing saw rapid increases in processing power over time. Quantum computing could have a similar effect on industries, helping to solve some of our biggest challenges, from discovering advanced materials to handling environmental issues that are currently hard to address. Recognizing and understanding exponential growth helps us prepare for the significant changes that quantum computing and similar technologies could bring.

However, it's important to note that exponential growth in qubit count doesn't mean a universal exponential speedup. Quantum computers excel at specific tasks such as factoring large numbers or simulating quantum systems, where they can leverage this parallelism for significant speedups. For other tasks, classical computers may still handle operations more efficiently.

Grasping exponential growth is also challenging due to what's called **exponential growth bias**. People generally think in linear terms, where changes happen in predictable, steady steps. This bias means we often underestimate just how quickly exponential growth can multiply power or impact. Research in Psychological Science even shows that most people find it easier to work with linear growth models, which can lead to underestimating how quickly technology can accelerate when exponential factors are at play.

Quantum computing, much like the early days of classical computing, could grow in leaps rather than small steps. With each new qubit added and improvements in error correction, quantum computers may eventually take on tasks that traditional machines cannot. This progress could make it possible to solve problems once considered out of reach, extending what we currently see as limits.

Quantum computing today

Quantum computing has come a long way in recent years. Once just a theoretical concept, it now includes real machines, cloud platforms, and even the controversial concept of **quantum supremacy** which we'll explain in more detail later which is when a quantum computer achieves something that a classical computer cannot accomplish in a reasonable timeframe.

Current quantum computers

Current quantum computers are more similar to scientific laboratories than conventional machines. They require carefully controlled environments, often operating near absolute zero, to keep qubits stable and reduce interference. These extreme conditions are necessary to make use of quantum effects like superposition and entanglement. While they aren't general-purpose computers, they are already being used for specific tasks that push beyond the limits of classical systems.

Among today's leading quantum computers is IBM's Eagle processor, featuring 127 qubits. Designed for complex calculations, Eagle excels at tasks that classical computers struggle with, such as simulating molecular structures in chemistry. This capability could accelerate advancements in fields like drug discovery and materials science.

Quantum Computing Inc. (QCI) takes a different approach, developing hybrid quantum-classical algorithms tailored for practical applications. By integrating quantum processors with classical resources, QCI aims to make quantum computing relevant to real-world optimization challenges.

Xanadu's quantum system, "Borealis", represents another innovative approach, using photonic technology (light particles instead of traditional qubit methods) to perform quantum calculations. Xanadu's focus on continuous-variable quantum computing opens new possibilities in **machine learning (ML)** and optimization, offering an alternative path to quantum advancements.

While these quantum systems are impressive, they remain delicate and specialized, excelling in areas that leverage quantum properties but still far from replacing everyday computers. For now, they serve as experimental tools, offering scientists and engineers a glimpse into the far-reaching potential of quantum computing in the future.

Current research projects

As quantum computing advances, collaborative research projects are forming worldwide, pooling expertise and resources from leading institutions to drive both theoretical and practical breakthroughs. One prominent initiative is the IBM Quantum Network, a global alliance connecting research institutions and companies to IBM's quantum computers. This network encourages collaboration over multiple industries, providing participants with access to IBM's quantum hardware and expertise. By facilitating experimental studies and applied research, the IBM Quantum Network helps accelerate development and test real-world applications that could shape future technologies.

Universities are also central to quantum research efforts. The **Massachusetts Institute of Technology (MIT)**, for example, hosts multiple initiatives focused on quantum information science, addressing challenges in algorithm development and hardware innovation. MIT's work supports advancements in cryptography and communication, laying the foundations for more secure data systems and efficient information transfer.

In Sweden, the **Wallenberg Centre for Quantum Technology (WACQT)** at Chalmers University of Technology is leading a national effort to advance quantum technology. Backed by 12 years of funding totaling around $100 million, WACQT aims to build a 100-qubit quantum computer capable of solving problems beyond what today's classical supercomputers can handle. The team is developing its own quantum processors using superconducting circuits, focusing on making qubits more reliable, reducing errors, and scaling up the system. This project places WACQT among the few research centers worldwide working toward a fully functional quantum computer.

As shown in the image below of the Chalmers researchers' cryostat, a quantum computer looks nothing like an ordinary silicon-based machine. Instead, it resembles something out of science fiction, with its intricate design and futuristic components built to function at extremely low temperatures.

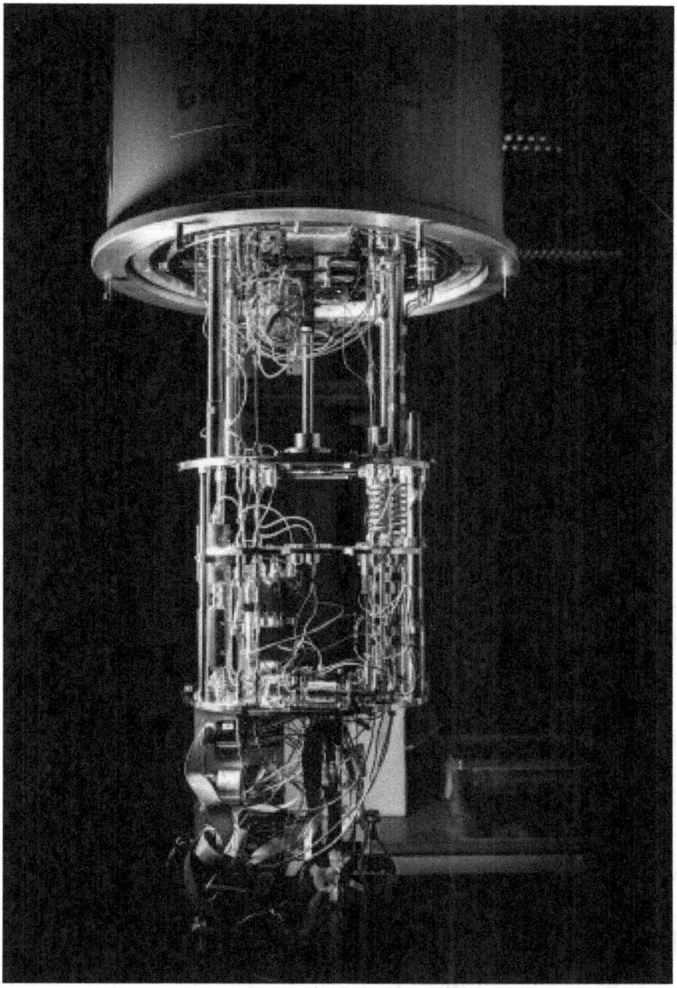

Photo by Johan Bodell

Outside of hardware, WACQT is working on quantum communication, quantum sensing, and quantum simulation. This includes developing secure communication methods and improving measurement precision for scientific and industrial use. WACQT collaborates with Swedish universities such as KTH Royal Institute of Technology and Lund University, along with international partners, to bring together expertise and drive progress. By combining advanced research with practical applications, WACQT aims to strengthen Sweden's role in quantum technology.

Collaborative projects, such as WACQT at Chalmers University and quantum research at MIT, show how shared resources and expertise help move the field forward. These efforts lay the groundwork for future discoveries that could have far-reaching effects.

Quantum supremacy

The term quantum supremacy refers to the point when a quantum computer achieves something that a classical computer cannot accomplish in a reasonable timeframe.

In 2019, Google's Sycamore processor marked a major milestone by completing a computation in minutes that, according to Google, would take classical supercomputers thousands of years. This event underscored the unique capability of quantum technology to handle specific tasks at speeds far out of the range of classical machines. Sycamore's achievement involved a problem specifically designed for quantum processing, generating and measuring a complex distribution of random numbers. While this experiment wasn't aimed at solving a practical, real-world problem, it showed that quantum computers could far exceed classical ones on certain types of computations, marking a leap in what's possible.

Related to quantum supremacy is the concept of **quantum advantage**, which describes instances where a quantum computer outperforms classical systems in practical applications, though not to the extreme extent seen in supremacy. While supremacy refers to a clear and dramatic computational victory over classical systems, quantum advantage focuses on situations where quantum systems show real, measurable benefits for specific tasks. This can occur even when the speedup is less dramatic than that seen in the Sycamore experiment. As quantum technology advances, quantum advantage is becoming more attainable for practical tasks, providing benefits in areas like optimization, simulation, and machine learning.

Other efforts have continued to explore this promising potential. In 2021, IBM introduced its **Quantum Hummingbird** processor, a 65-qubit system, demonstrating that it could solve certain optimization problems in quantum chemistry simulations faster than classical computers. These early results hint at practical applications coming closer to reality, showing that quantum advancements are moving beyond theory.

Fujitsu's Digital Annealer, while not a true quantum computer, applies quantum-inspired methods to solve intricate optimization problems. In 2020, it outperformed classical computers in logistics and supply chain scenarios, demonstrating that even quantum-inspired systems can offer valuable solutions for real-world problems.

Similarly, **D-Wave Systems** has achieved notable results with its quantum annealers. In 2020, D-Wave's system efficiently optimized a traffic flow problem, completing the task faster than classical approaches and suggesting that quantum-inspired technology holds practical value in solving everyday issues.

Further expanding the concept of quantum supremacy, research into **quantum random walks** has demonstrated potential. In classical computing, a "random walk" is a process that simulates a path made up of a series of random steps (like someone taking unpredictable steps in different directions). This method is often used to model behaviors in finance, physics, and other fields. In quantum random walks, however, quantum particles can exist in multiple states simultaneously, allowing them to "walk" in multiple directions at once because of quantum superposition. This unique property enables quantum random walks to explore pathways more efficiently than classical random walks, making them faster for certain search tasks. A 2020 study found that quantum random walks could handle specific search tasks more effectively than classical methods, illustrating yet another way quantum technology is pushing the boundaries of computation.

These examples highlight how quantum technology is exceeding the capabilities of classical systems, unlocking new potential across various fields.

The significance of quantum supremacy lies in its demonstration of what quantum systems can achieve, although this doesn't mean quantum computers will universally surpass classical ones. Instead, quantum supremacy is task-specific, addressing scenarios where classical methods reach their limits. Quantum computers currently excel in areas with extreme data demands, and while the technology is still developing, specific tasks are showing the impact of quantum's unique capabilities.

One area where quantum computing offers opportunities is in quantum simulations. Quantum systems can model certain quantum environments, like high-temperature superconductors or complex molecular interactions crucial for drug discovery, more effectively than classical computers. By simulating these interactions, quantum computing opens new possibilities in materials science and medicine, offering insights into phenomena that would otherwise remain out of reach.

Another potential use for quantum computing lies in solving intricate optimization problems. Quantum algorithms have shown potential in logistics, identifying optimal routes and managing resources with precision to enhance operational efficiency. These capabilities show how quantum systems can tackle real-world problems that involve many variables and constraints, particularly in areas like supply chain management.

Machine learning is also set to benefit from quantum advancements. Though still in the early stages, quantum computing could speed up the processing of large datasets, enhancing machine learning and boosting AI-driven tasks. With ongoing development, quantum computing may ultimately improve predictive models and accelerate data analysis, bringing greater efficiency to businesses.

These advances in quantum simulation, optimization, and early-stage machine learning illustrate how quantum systems are complementing classical computing. While current use remains focused on specialized tasks, each step forward shows quantum computing's ability to solve today's pressing problems, offering glimpses of a future where it becomes a vital tool throughout multiple fields.

As quantum computing progresses, researchers and organizations are expected to pursue more applications that show its potential. Each advancement not only reinforces the foundations of quantum computing but also moves us closer to practical applications across enterprises. While the full scope of quantum computing is still being realized, the movement toward quantum supremacy has already changed our understanding of what's possible with computation and its role in shaping the future.

Quantum computing in the cloud

Quantum computing has come a long way from its beginnings as a field confined to academic labs and theoretical discussions. Initially, it was considered an area of pure research, with real applications seeming distant and almost out of reach. Now, through **Quantum-as-a-Service (QaaS)** platforms, quantum computing has entered a new era of accessibility. Just a few years ago, direct access to quantum hardware through the cloud wasn't even conceivable. Platforms like **Amazon Braket**, **Microsoft**

Azure Quantum, and **IBM Quantum Platform** are not only bridging the gap between theory and experimentation but are doing so in a way that would have been unimaginable in the early days of quantum mechanics. The rapid pace of development has turned what was once confined to specialized labs into a resource accessible to anyone with an internet connection.

These platforms serve a diverse range of users, from beginners and students to researchers and industry professionals, demonstrating the flexibility and broad appeal of cloud-based quantum computing. For those new to the field, QaaS offers an entry point to test quantum principles, explore algorithms, and learn foundational concepts without needing access to expensive or complex hardware. Meanwhile, experienced researchers and professionals can use these services to run sophisticated experiments and solve specific problems, from simulating chemical reactions to optimizing logistics networks. QaaS essentially adapts to the skill level of its users, making it a versatile tool that caters to a wide audience.

Amazon Braket, for example, provides access to quantum processors from firms such as IonQ, **Rigetti**, and D-Wave. Named after a notation in quantum mechanics, Amazon Braket acts as a "library" of quantum resources. Each processor on the platform is tailored to a different task. IonQ's trapped-ion qubits are recognized for their stability, ideal for tasks that demand high precision. On the other hand, D-Wave's quantum annealers are designed to address optimization problems, making them suitable for scenarios like network logistics. Users can select the processor that best matches their requirements, whether they need accuracy for chemical simulations or optimization capabilities for complex logistical challenges.

Microsoft Azure Quantum also provides access to quantum computing resources through partnerships with companies such as IonQ and Honeywell. This platform offers an integrated approach, combining quantum hardware with Microsoft's classical computing resources. This hybrid setup supports the creation of algorithms that blend both quantum and classical computing techniques. For instance, a logistics company might handle everyday processes with classical computing and use Microsoft Azure Quantum to optimize high-level decisions that require the unique strengths of quantum processors.

IBM Quantum Platform broadens access to quantum technology further by offering both free and paid options to explore IBM's quantum processors. The platform includes IBM's powerful 127-qubit Eagle processor, allowing users to interact with quantum hardware in real-time. It's an especially valuable entry point for students, researchers, and enthusiasts, as the IBM Quantum Platform also provides educational resources and a community forum where users can share insights and support each other's learning. This approach, similar to open-source software communities, accelerates progress by encouraging collaboration, with users able to share knowledge, troubleshoot, and explore together.

These QaaS platforms also offer unique flexibility by allowing users to experiment with a range of hardware and software combinations. Whether someone wants to work with different types of quantum processors or test hybrid algorithms, QaaS supports a tailored approach to quantum exploration. By providing quantum simulators alongside actual quantum hardware, these platforms make it possible to move from simple quantum tasks, like simulating coin flips, to more sophisticated algorithm testing, making quantum computing a flexible and accessible field.

Hybrid quantum-classical systems are an important step in advancing quantum computing's practical applications. These systems combine the strengths of quantum processors, which excel at certain specialized calculations, with the reliability and speed of classical computers for tasks like data preprocessing and iterative refinement. A prime example of this synergy is the **Quantum Approximate Optimization Algorithm (QAOA)**. In QAOA, the quantum computer evaluates potential solutions to an optimization problem while the classical computer adjusts the parameters to improve outcomes. This back-and-forth process between the quantum and classical components allows the system to refine solutions iteratively, balancing the unique advantages of each type of processor.

Such hybrid models are valuable for optimization problems, where many variables and constraints must be considered simultaneously. QAOA and similar algorithms have already proven effective at improving efficiency and providing solutions beyond the reach of classical methods alone. By enabling quantum and classical processors to work together, hybrid systems not only make the most of current quantum hardware but also offer a glimpse into how quantum computing may become integral to solving real-world problems.

This alternate approach to quantum computing has democratized access to what was once highly specialized technology. Today, thanks to QaaS, the world of quantum computing is open to a broader audience than ever before. While quantum computers aren't yet ready to replace classical machines, they are already showing their strengths in certain areas and setting the stage for more advanced applications. The achievement of quantum supremacy has shown that quantum processors can outperform classical ones on specific tasks, and the cloud has brought these possibilities closer to researchers, learners, and innovators worldwide.

Timeline of key quantum milestones

The story of quantum computing is filled with important breakthroughs, each one expanding our understanding and capabilities. Starting with early theories and leading to today's cloud-based Quantum-as-a-Service platforms, each milestone has moved quantum computing closer to practical use. This timeline shows how quantum computing has developed from an idea into an accessible technology, capturing the key achievements that have brought us to where we are today and hinting at what might be possible in the future.

1900 Planck's Quantum Hypothesis: Max Planck introduces the concept of quantized energy, laying the groundwork for quantum mechanics.

1905 Einstein's Photoelectric Effect: Albert Einstein explains the photoelectric effect by proposing light comprises quantized packets, or "photons", earning him the Nobel Prize and advancing quantum theory.

1925-1927 Foundations of Quantum Mechanics: Werner Heisenberg, Erwin Schrödinger, and Paul Dirac establish quantum mechanics, introducing concepts like wave functions and uncertainty. Schrödinger's wave equation becomes central to describing quantum systems.

1935 EPR Paradox and Quantum Entanglement: Einstein, Podolsky, and Rosen introduce the **"spooky action at a distance"** concept, questioning quantum mechanics' completeness and introducing quantum entanglement.

1964 Bell's Theorem: John Bell shows quantum mechanics predicts quantum entanglement-based correlations that classical physics cannot explain, paving the way for future experiments in quantum entanglement.

1981 Feynman's Quantum Computing Concept: Richard Feynman proposes quantum computers as a way to simulate quantum physics, highlighting classical computers' limitations in modeling quantum systems.

1985 Deutsch's Universal Quantum Computer: David Deutsch formalizes the idea of a universal quantum computer capable of performing any computational task.

1994 Shor's Algorithm: Peter Shor develops an algorithm for efficiently factoring large numbers on a quantum computer, revealing quantum computing's potential to challenge classical cryptography.

1997 Quantum Teleportation Demonstrated: Anton Zeilinger's team achieved the first successful **quantum teleportation** of information, proving the feasibility of information transfer through quantum entanglement.

2001 First Quantum Algorithm on NMR Quantum Computer: IBM and Stanford researchers implement Shor's algorithm on a 7-qubit nuclear magnetic resonance (NMR) quantum computer, marking early quantum computing achievements.

2011 D-Wave Introduces Commercial Quantum Computer: D-Wave Systems launches the D-Wave One, a 128-qubit quantum annealer, marking the first commercial quantum computing system.

2013 Google and NASA Collaborate on Quantum Computing: Google, NASA, and USRA establish the Quantum AI Lab and install a D-Wave Two system at NASA Ames to study quantum annealing for tasks like optimization and machine learning.

2017 IBM Q Network and 20-Qubit Processor: IBM launches the IBM Q Network, providing cloud access to a 20-qubit quantum computer, broadening access for researchers and developers worldwide.

2018 Google Bristlecone (72 Qubits): Google unveils Bristlecone, a 72-qubit processor aimed at achieving quantum supremacy.

2019 Google Achieves Quantum Supremacy: Google's 54-qubit Sycamore processor completes a computation in 200 seconds, which would take classical supercomputers thousands of years, marking quantum supremacy for a specific task.

2021 IBM's Eagle Processor (127 Qubits): IBM announces Eagle, a 127-qubit processor, representing a leap in qubit count and computational complexity.

2022 Xanadu's Borealis and Quantum Advantage: Xanadu's Borealis, a photonic quantum computer, performs a sampling task beyond the capabilities of classical computers, achieving quantum advantage.

2023 IBM's Condor (433 Qubits) and Quantum Roadmap: IBM unveils its 433-qubit Condor chip and announces plans to develop systems with over 1,000 qubits, aiming toward fault-tolerant quantum computing.

This timeline captures the evolution of quantum mechanics from foundational discoveries to groundbreaking technological achievements, highlighting key milestones that have advanced our understanding and capability in quantum computing.

BEYOND TODAY

Part II

The intersection of AI and quantum computing

As quantum computing advances, one of its most promising partnerships is with AI. To understand the potential of this AI-quantum synergy, it helps to first look at AI's foundations and how it functions. Quantum computing and AI each offer distinct strengths, and together, they could achieve outcomes beyond what either could accomplish alone. AI has already reshaped industries by analyzing data, making predictions, and automating tasks. Quantum computing could push AI further, enhancing its ability to perform data-heavy calculations that would otherwise take too much time. In return, AI could accelerate progress in quantum computing by refining algorithms, managing complex datasets, and even contributing to the design of quantum hardware.

AI, in simple terms, is a technology that enables machines to perform tasks that require human intelligence such as recognizing patterns, solving intricate problems, deciding, and creating original content. Understanding AI's key areas and applications helps reveal where quantum computing could play a role in advancing this technology.

One area where quantum computing could support AI is in processing power. Training large AI models requires substantial computing resources, especially for tasks like speech recognition, which involves analyzing extensive audio data to learn distinct patterns and accents. This process consumes significant energy. For instance, training **OpenAI's** GPT-3, a large language model, used approximately 1,287 megawatt-hours (MWh) of electricity; about the same amount consumed annually by 120 average U.S. households. As AI models grow in size and complexity, their energy demands increase accordingly. Quantum computing, with its ability to process multiple possibilities simultaneously, could reduce the time and energy needed for these calculations, potentially making future AI systems faster and more energy-efficient.

AI could also advance quantum computing. Quantum research often involves managing large datasets, such as tracking qubit stability and analyzing error rates. AI algorithms can play a key role by identifying patterns in this data, suggesting improvements in quantum circuit designs, and predicting errors in real-time. A **quantum circuit** is a sequence of operations applied to qubits to perform a specific computation, similar to how classical circuits process bits in traditional computing. In this way, AI helps researchers improve quantum computing performance and increase system reliability.

Together, quantum computing and AI could lead to innovations that address some of society's most pressing issues.

Understanding the basics of AI and machine learning

AI aims to create systems that can handle tasks traditionally done by people, such as reasoning, learning, and problem-solving. Conventional programming involves giving computers explicit instructions for each action. But AI takes a different approach, it allows machines to learn and adapt based on data and experience. Machine learning, a popular method in AI, enables this adaptability by letting algorithms analyze large datasets, uncover patterns, and make decisions, predictions, or classifications.

Machine learning typically involves three main approaches. In **supervised learning**, models are trained on labeled data, where each data point includes the correct answer. For instance, a model might use thousands of labeled images to learn how to identify cats. By recognizing patterns in these examples, the model learns to make accurate predictions for new, unlabeled data.

In **unsupervised learning**, the model works with data that has no labels. The aim here is for the AI system to uncover patterns, groupings, or structures within the data on its own. A common use is in customer segmentation, where companies can group customers with similar purchasing habits based on analyzed data.

Reinforcement learning, another approach, teaches the AI through a trial-and-error process. The AI receives rewards or penalties based on its actions, learning over time to make decisions that lead to better outcomes. This approach is often applied in fields like robotics or gaming, where an agent can explore various strategies and learn from its successes and failures.

Deep learning and neural networks

Deep learning, a specialized field within machine learning, is behind many of AI's major advancements. Built on artificial **neural networks** inspired by the structure of the human brain, deep learning uses layers of nodes to process data in stages. Each layer identifies patterns, passing information to the next layer for further refinement, enabling deep learning models to uncover complex patterns and relationships within data.

Some of the primary applications of deep learning include image and speech recognition. This technology has made it possible for machines to interpret visual and audio inputs with high accuracy. Tools like facial recognition, virtual assistants (such as Siri), and real-time language translation all depend on advancements in neural networks to function effectively.

Another key application is **natural language processing (NLP)**, which enables AI to understand and generate human language. NLP supports a range of tools, including chatbots, translation software, and sentiment analysis, which involves identifying emotions or opinions expressed in text, such as whether a review is positive or negative. With ongoing advancements, NLP allows AI systems to engage in meaningful conversations and create coherent text, significantly broadening AI's potential in communication and content generation.

Generative AI

Generative AI is an impressive branch of artificial intelligence that allows machines to create new content, such as text, images, music, or video. These models are trained on large datasets and use pattern recognition to produce outputs that often resemble human creativity. In practical terms, this means that an AI can write an article, generate a photorealistic image, compose music, or even mimic a person's voice.

The technology behind generative AI is undeniably powerful. It has already changed how people create and interact with digital content, opening up possibilities in design, entertainment, education, and research. Tools like ChatGPT, DALL-E, Midjourney, and others have shown that machines can now produce work that is sometimes indistinguishable from what a human might create.

Generative AI relies on models such as:

- **Generative adversarial networks (GANs):** GANs consist of two neural networks (a generator and a discriminator) that work against each other. The generator creates new data, while the discriminator assesses it, providing feedback to refine the generator's output. GANs are widely used for generating realistic images, art, and simulations.

- **Transformers and large language models (LLMs):** Transformers are a neural network architecture especially effective in natural language processing (NLP). Large language models, like GPT (Generative Pre-trained Transformer), are popular for generating human-like text and are used for tasks like content creation, code generation, and language translation.

The rapid progress of Generative AI comes with serious questions. Most generative AI systems are trained on data collected from the internet. Text, images, and other media that were often created by people who never gave permission for their work to be used. This has led to widespread criticism, especially from artists, writers, and creators whose work has been copied, imitated, or reused without credit or compensation.

In one widely shared article, a developer who spent years working on generative AI now calls the practice "theft," pointing out that these models rely on the unpaid labor of millions of people whose content forms the backbone of the training data. The New York Times has taken legal action against OpenAI, claiming that its copyrighted material was used without permission to train language models. Other lawsuits are underway from visual artists, authors, and software developers who argue that their work has been scraped and reused without consent.

There's also a broader cultural concern. If machines are trained to imitate human creativity using past human output, what happens to the value of original work? What does it mean to create something "new" when the training process is based entirely on existing material? These are open questions, and society is only beginning to reckon with them.

Generative AI is a major technological achievement, but it sits at the center of a growing debate about ownership, creativity, and fairness. As the field continues to develop, it will be important not only to focus on what these systems can do, but also to consider how they're built, whose work they depend on, and who benefits from their output.

Where AI stands today

AI is already making a major impact in different fields. In healthcare, it supports diagnostics and analyzes patient data. In finance, it helps detect fraud and optimize investment strategies. In retail, AI enables personalized recommendations and streamlines inventory management.

However, AI still faces some challenges. Traditional AI systems often struggle with tasks that require deep reasoning or a firm grasp of complex context. Additionally, training AI models demands large amounts of data, which can lead to biased results if the data is not diverse or well-represented.

Another limitation is the substantial processing power required for training and deploying advanced AI models. For example, training a deep learning model can take days or weeks on standard computers, especially with large datasets. This is where quantum computing could eventually make a difference by significantly improving the speed and efficiency of AI's data processing abilities.

How quantum could supercharge AI

Quantum computing offers unique capabilities that address several limitations in AI, particularly in areas requiring intensive computation, optimization, and pattern recognition.

With its ability to perform complex calculations simultaneously, quantum computing enhances AI's computational power. This capability allows AI systems to process larger datasets faster than classical computers can manage. Healthcare, for instance, is one field where quantum-powered AI could enable real-time analysis of patient data, supporting quicker diagnoses and more tailored treatment plans.

Quantum computing also excels at optimization, a critical component in training machine learning models. Solving complicated optimization problems efficiently helps AI find better solutions in less time. This advantage is especially useful in logistics, where quantum-powered AI could refine supply chain management by analyzing a broader range of variables and constraints than classical AI can handle.

Additionally, quantum computing could enhance deep learning by speeding up pattern recognition for large datasets. Neural networks rely heavily on data and processing power, and quantum systems make it possible to analyze these patterns more efficiently. This improvement could allow AI to handle more intricate visual data, boosting image recognition tasks and enabling the management of more complex data spanning multiple industries.

Quantum Machine Learning (QML)

Quantum Machine Learning (QML) is a relatively new area that focuses on creating AI models specifically designed for quantum hardware, taking advantage of the unique properties of quantum computing. The goal of QML is to build AI models that not only run faster but can also perform tasks beyond the reach of classical AI.

Some early QML models have great potential, especially in multifaceted tasks like pattern recognition and data classification. By using quantum properties like superposition, these models can explore multiple solutions at once. In drug discovery, for example, QML could allow AI to analyze a large number of molecular combinations more quickly, predicting how different drugs might interact at the atomic level with greater precision. This approach could apply to designing new drugs, analyzing genetic data, or predicting protein structures in biomedicine.

Although QML is still in its early stages, the field is advancing rapidly. Most algorithms are currently under research, with efforts focused on improving their accuracy, stability, and compatibility with quantum hardware. As quantum computers continue to develop, QML is expected to play an increasingly significant role in advancing AI capabilities in various fields.

Challenges and limitations with Quantum-AI integration

Integrating quantum computing with today's AI systems comes with several practical challenges. Quantum computers process data differently from classical systems, making it necessary to rethink how AI tools like TensorFlow and PyTorch, which are optimized for CPUs and GPUs, can interact with quantum hardware. To address this, entirely new frameworks must be developed to allow classical and quantum systems to work together seamlessly. These frameworks will require innovative programming methods, better data management, and expertise spanning both fields to bridge the gap effectively.

There's also a need to build a workforce with a unique set of skills. Just as software engineering developed to blend hardware, programming, and DevOps knowledge, working with quantum-AI systems will require knowledge of quantum mechanics, AI, data science, and algorithm design. However, this skill combination is still rare, so there's a growing need for education and training programs that can equip professionals for these specialized roles.

Ensuring data accuracy in quantum-AI systems is another key issue. Quantum data processing is very sensitive to interference from factors like temperature and electromagnetic fields, which can introduce errors. In areas that demand high accuracy, error correction is critical. Classical systems often handle this through redundant data, but quantum systems need new error correction methods since quantum data can't be copied exactly. Researchers are currently developing methods to improve accuracy in these systems.

Scaling quantum-AI applications is also challenging. Today's quantum computers are limited in size, with the most advanced systems containing only around 100 to 400 qubits, whereas many AI applications require much more power to handle millions of parameters, such as those used in image recognition or natural language processing. In the short term, a combined approach where quantum and classical systems work together will likely be needed, with each handling the parts they're best suited for. To make this work, we'll need stronger quantum hardware and new ways of designing AI models that effectively use both systems.

Managing energy demands is another important consideration. Many quantum computers use superconducting qubits, which need extremely low temperatures to function, making them energy-intensive. This makes quantum computing less energy-efficient than classical computing for now. Researchers are exploring alternatives like photonic qubits, which can work at room temperature, to create more energy-efficient quantum systems and make their use in AI more sustainable.

Overcoming these obstacles will require collaboration across disciplines, continuous technological advancements, and the development of new tools and frameworks. As these hurdles are gradually addressed, integrating quantum computing and AI will become more practical, laying the groundwork for new types of applications.

Quantum applications across industries

Quantum computing is already being explored for problems that overwhelm classical systems, especially those involving many interacting variables.

This part of the book explores how quantum computing is beginning to make an impact, focusing on its current applications and future possibilities across industries such as *science and healthcare*, *finance and security*, *infrastructure and planning*, and advanced technologies like *space exploration*.

Quantum computing in science and healthcare

In science and healthcare, quantum computing offers remarkable possibilities to advance discovery and improve the delivery of care. By enabling precision molecular simulations, it could speed up drug development, while advanced climate modeling may deepen our understanding of the natural world. This technology opens the door to innovations that can lead to better medical treatments, sustainable environmental solutions, and more accurate scientific insights.

Healthcare and drug discovery

In the future, treatments for diseases like cancer or Alzheimer's could be developed as precisely as matching a key to a lock, tailored to each patient's unique biology. Quantum computing might make this possible by simulating molecular interactions with extraordinary accuracy, accelerating the path from discovery to cure.

Healthcare and drug discovery are critical to modern society, impacting billions of lives and generating over a trillion dollars annually for fields like pharmaceuticals, diagnostics, biotechnology, and genomics. While these areas drive major advances in public health, developing new treatments remains a lengthy and expensive process, often taking over a decade and requiring significant financial investment. Only a small fraction of potential drugs ultimately reach approval. Pharmaceutical companies spend billions each year to test compounds, screen potential therapies, and meet regulatory requirements, but with success rates near just 10%, more efficient methods are needed. Quantum computing, combined with AI, could improve drug discovery by lowering costs and enabling more personalized treatments.

The innovation landscape in healthcare is supported by a collaborative network of pharmaceutical companies, biotech firms, and research institutions. Industry leaders like Pfizer, Merck, and AstraZeneca focus on conditions such as cancer and cardiovascular disease. With their financial resources, infrastructure, and expertise, these companies can adopt advanced technologies early, leveraging AI and quantum computing to enhance drug development. This includes identifying promising compounds, simulating molecular interactions, and optimizing clinical trials. Biotech companies like Moderna and Regeneron, known for their work on mRNA vaccines and gene therapies, are also exploring quantum technology to simulate molecular interactions, potentially speeding up the drug development process while increasing accuracy.

During the COVID-19 pandemic, the accelerated development of vaccines demonstrated the critical need for faster, more adaptable drug discovery methods. Quantum computing could enhance the speed of such responses by efficiently simulating molecular interactions, potentially helping researchers identify effective treatments and vaccines more rapidly in future health crises.

Academic and research institutions, including MIT, Harvard, and the Broad Institute, conduct studies that advance medical science. These institutions often work with tech companies to explore quantum applications in molecular modeling and genetics, aiming to gain deeper insights into disease mechanisms and potential treatments. Quantum-focused startups like Qubit Pharmaceuticals and **Quantinuum** bring specialized quantum knowledge into healthcare, partnering with established pharmaceutical companies to speed up molecular simulations and early-stage drug discovery through quantum algorithms.

Regulatory bodies like the U.S. Food and Drug Administration (FDA), the World Health Organization (WHO), and the Centers for Disease Control and Prevention (CDC) play an essential role in ensuring new therapies are safe and effective. As quantum technology becomes further integrated into drug development, these agencies may need to adapt their frameworks to assess quantum-assisted drug approval processes, ensuring that innovations meet necessary public health standards.

Drug development is often compared to finding a needle in a haystack, where researchers identify promising compounds and conduct years of testing to ensure their safety and effectiveness. This process involves analyzing molecular interactions and conducting preclinical and clinical trials, with costs frequently reaching billions of dollars for a single drug. Diseases such as cancer and Alzheimer's require an in-depth understanding of genetic and molecular factors, while the rise of antibiotic-resistant bacteria and fast-mutating viruses, as seen with COVID-19, calls for adaptable solutions.

Quantum computing, with its ability to simulate molecular interactions, can accelerate the early stages of drug discovery by predicting how compounds will bind to target proteins. This reduces the need for costly trial-and-error approaches in physical labs. Additionally, quantum algorithms can analyze large chemical datasets to identify patterns and relationships that might be overlooked by classical methods, helping researchers discover new drug candidates more efficiently. Combined with AI, quantum computing can also refine clinical trial design by modeling potential outcomes and optimizing patient selection, improving the likelihood of success. These capabilities, alongside other advanced technologies like AI-driven protein modeling and genomic analysis, could significantly reduce the time and cost of bringing effective drugs to market.

Among recent breakthroughs, Google DeepMind's **AlphaFold** stands out as an AI tool that predicts the 3D structures of proteins, greatly accelerating research by providing fast, accurate models of protein shapes. This capability has been likened to opening up a huge biological puzzle, as understanding a protein's shape can reveal its function and interactions with other molecules which is vital for studying diseases. In recognition of this achievement, Demis Hassabis and John Jumper were awarded the 2024 Nobel Prize in Chemistry for their work on AlphaFold.

However, AlphaFold provides static images of proteins, showing them in fixed positions rather than in the constantly changing environments within the body. Here, quantum computing could enhance AlphaFold's impact by introducing dynamic simulations that model how proteins fold and adapt in real-time. This added layer of insight could help researchers understand processes like protein misfolding, which is linked to conditions such as Parkinson's disease, providing a more detailed view of disease mechanisms.

Quantum computing is also suited to simulating drug interactions with proteins in real-time, allowing researchers to see how drug molecules bind to target proteins. While AlphaFold gives a static snapshot, quantum technology could reveal how proteins behave dynamically, aiding in the faster identification of promising drug candidates. This capability could ultimately help accelerate the drug discovery process by providing a more comprehensive view of molecular interactions.

Precision medicine, an approach that tailors treatments to each individual's genetic profile, lifestyle, and environment, could benefit significantly from quantum computing's power to simulate genetic interactions. This approach moves beyond one-size-fits-all treatments, allowing doctors to create therapies that align with each patient's unique biology. For example, by using quantum-powered genomic analysis, researchers can identify specific mutations linked to diseases like cancer, leading to targeted therapies. Notable organizations such as Quantinuum and AstraZeneca are actively developing quantum algorithms to identify disease-linked genetic mutations, with the goal of supporting personalized interventions to improve patient outcomes.

Quantum computing's potential in preventive medicine is another promising area. By analyzing extensive datasets on genetic profiles, lifestyle habits, and environmental influences, quantum algorithms could help create detailed risk profiles, enabling healthcare providers to anticipate health issues before they become critical. This preventive approach could even extend to mental health, where quantum models might analyze genetic tendencies and behavior patterns to estimate the likelihood of conditions like depression.

As quantum computing and AI combine to make healthcare more precise and proactive, data security becomes a critical priority. The sensitive nature of genetic and medical information requires strong encryption, and quantum-safe methods are essential for protecting this data. These techniques allow researchers, clinicians, and patients to collaborate safely, ensuring privacy and integrity in the handling of sensitive information.

One of the most promising applications of quantum-powered AI is in real-time analysis of patient data. By leveraging quantum computing's ability to process complex datasets and AI's predictive capabilities, healthcare systems could deliver quicker diagnoses and more personalized treatments. For example, researchers at IBM and partnerships like those between Quantinuum and pharmaceutical companies are already exploring how quantum-enhanced AI algorithms could analyze health data to detect early warning signs of diseases such as heart conditions or infections. These systems could monitor patients continuously, flagging subtle changes that might indicate complications before they become critical.

Real-time analysis could also revolutionize emergency care. Say we have an AI system, supported by quantum computing, processing live data from wearable devices, medical imaging, and electronic health records to guide doctors in making faster, more accurate decisions during critical situations. This capability would allow healthcare providers to respond more effectively, reducing treatment delays and improving outcomes.

As this technology progresses, its integration into preventive medicine could help identify patterns in genetic, lifestyle, and environmental factors that contribute to diseases. This proactive approach would shift healthcare from treating illnesses to predicting and preventing them. For instance, quantum-powered AI could analyze genetic markers to assess cancer risks or combine real-time patient monitoring with environmental data to predict asthma exacerbations.

With its ability to model genetic interactions, predict treatment responses, and integrate real-time patient data, quantum computing could bring healthcare closer to a truly personalized model. Soon, doctors might not only tailor treatments to each individual's biology but also predict and prevent health crises with unparalleled accuracy. This proactive, data-driven era is positioned to enhance accessibility, privacy, and effectiveness in healthcare, offering new ways to improve both individual outcomes and global health systems.

The combined power of AI and quantum computing has the potential to change healthcare, making it more responsive, adaptable, and capable of addressing the unique needs of every patient while supporting broader public health initiatives. This collaborative technology could lay the ground for a future where healthcare systems work seamlessly to save lives and improve well-being.

Materials science and smart manufacturing

What if new materials could be designed in days instead of years, with properties perfectly suited for electric cars, renewable energy, or lightweight airplanes? Quantum computing might unlock this future by revealing the secrets of matter at the atomic level.

Materials science and smart manufacturing are key drivers of innovation for sectors like electronics, transportation, healthcare, and renewable energy. However, these fields face significant difficulties. Accurately simulating material properties is a major issue, as traditional computers struggle to model the atomic and molecular interactions that dictate how materials behave. Manufacturing processes, meanwhile, often require large amounts of energy and produce considerable waste, creating a strong push for more sustainable methods that minimize resource use. Stricter environmental regulations and the high cost of rare materials add to the urgency for alternative solutions that are both effective and accessible. Trial-and-error approaches in manufacturing further contribute to inefficiencies, highlighting the need for more advanced tools.

Quantum computing offers promising solutions to many of these problems. By processing multiple possibilities simultaneously, quantum computers can simulate material interactions more quickly and accurately, accelerating the discovery of new compounds with desired properties such as strength, flexibility, and conductivity. These advances could make manufacturing processes more efficient while supporting sustainability goals.

Recent developments, such as lightweight alloys in aerospace and conductive polymers for flexible electronics, demonstrate how materials science continues to shape progress. Smart manufacturing builds on these advancements by aiming to boost efficiency, reduce waste, and meet modern environmental standards through optimized production methods.

Leading companies are now exploring quantum computing to further accelerate innovation in materials science and manufacturing. **BASF**, a global leader in chemical production, collaborates with quantum technology firms like **HQS Quantum Simulations** to speed up material discovery. Similarly, IBM and Google are advancing quantum simulations, with IBM targeting renewable energy applications and Google focusing on materials for next-generation batteries. Toyota is also investing in quantum research to improve electric vehicle battery performance and support sustainable manufacturing.

Startups such as Xanadu are at the forefront of quantum applications for materials science, particularly in developing algorithms to identify compounds for cleaner energy sources and more efficient solar cells. Research centers like the **National Renewable Energy Laboratory (NREL)** are teaming up with quantum research groups to create energy-efficient materials for solar power and battery technology. Universities like MIT and Quantinuum are leading simulations that explore molecular structures for potential applications in healthcare, electronics, and catalysis.

Quantum computing offers unique potential for materials science, as it can simulate atomic interactions with high precision, speeding up material discovery for applications like energy storage and transportation. For example, in developing electric vehicle batteries, quantum simulations can help test combinations of materials to find those with high energy density and stability, streamlining the development of efficient, long-lasting batteries. Quantum simulations also extend to finding efficient catalysts for carbon capture and discovering materials for renewable energy storage.

Quantum computing's impact on materials science goes beyond AI's role in the field. Quantum computers can simulate material interactions independently, allowing researchers to directly observe how materials respond under different conditions. In energy storage, this could lead to discovering compounds with higher charge capacity or faster charging times, offering clear benefits for electric vehicle technology and beyond.

Quantum technology also promises to make manufacturing greener. Quantum computers can simulate chemical reactions to identify catalysts that make production more energy-efficient, helping to lower emissions while reducing costs. BASF, for instance, collaborates with quantum research firms to explore how simulations can cut energy use in chemical production. These simulations could help energy-intensive industries, like steel and chemicals, operate more sustainably by reducing waste and optimizing resource use.

Quantum computing's detailed simulations of material interactions also have important real-world applications. In aerospace, for example, where materials must be both lightweight and durable, quantum simulations can help identify alloys and composites that meet high standards. Similarly, in automotive manufacturing, quantum simulations could lead to materials that make vehicles lighter and more fuel-efficient.

As the field of quantum computing develops, it will continue to support the discovery of sustainable materials suited to various sectors. Quantum simulations could enable materials that perform reliably under extreme conditions, such as heat-resistant composites for aerospace or climate-adapted construction materials for hot or rainy environments.

Overall, quantum computing can impact the future of materials science and manufacturing by allowing faster, more accurate simulations of atomic properties. This technology could lead to new materials, more efficient production methods, and sustainable practices that reduce energy consumption and environmental impact. As quantum technology advances, it will enhance the development and use of materials across multiple sectors, driving progress in ways that improve both performance and sustainability.

Climate science and environmental modeling

What if we could predict the path of a hurricane weeks ahead or model the effects of carbon capture systems with the accuracy of a fine-tuned instrument? Quantum computing could equip humanity with the tools to understand and protect our planet like never before.

Climate science and environmental modeling are key to understanding and addressing climate change. These efforts influence policies, public health initiatives, and disaster response strategies, impacting economies and societies worldwide. Trillions are being invested in renewable energy, emissions reduction, and climate adaptation. Reliable climate models, which rely on grand datasets like ocean currents, atmospheric conditions, and deforestation rates, are essential for predicting environmental changes and assessing risks. These include rising sea levels, extreme weather events, and biodiversity loss. Analyzing these interconnected factors requires immense computing power, as climate models must capture the detailed relationships between elements like temperature and ecosystem health.

Sweden, for instance, leads the way in climate resilience, drawing over 50% of its energy from renewable sources and aiming for carbon neutrality by 2045. Other countries, like Norway and Germany, are also heavily investing in sustainable technologies, each taking distinct approaches to managing their climate goals.

Despite this progress, there are limits to the accuracy and practical use of today's climate models. The sheer volume of data and the processing power needed are major hurdles. Climate models need to account for complex interactions, like how shifts in ocean temperatures affect weather patterns or how deforestation impacts carbon dioxide levels. Traditional computers process each detail step by step, a time-consuming method that can miss critical connections.

Modeling extreme events such as hurricanes, floods, and wildfires also presents unique challenges. These events demand highly accurate data and advanced modeling techniques, yet many current computational tools lack the speed and precision required for creating timely, practical forecasts. This limits their effectiveness in preparing for and responding to natural disasters. Additionally, integrating short-term and long-term data for comprehensive climate strategies requires significant effort and careful coordination. Immediate weather forecasts depend on short-term data, while long-term trends inform climate resilience planning. Combining data across these timescales calls for robust processing capabilities.

Recent technological advances in climate science are creating new opportunities for quantum computing to contribute meaningfully. Real-time satellite monitoring now allows for tracking environmental changes like rising sea levels, melting ice caps, and deforestation. Companies such as Planet Labs provide essential satellite data that aids conservation and shapes policy. With accurate, up-to-date imagery, governments and researchers can respond more effectively to environmental shifts.

AI and machine learning are increasingly integral to climate research. For instance, Google's DeepMind partnered with the UK Met Office to enhance short-term rainfall forecasting. Their AI model, trained on three years of UK radar data, was evaluated by over 50 expert meteorologists and outperformed existing methods in 89% of cases for accuracy and usefulness. This advancement in "nowcasting", predicting weather in the immediate future, offers improved early warnings for severe weather events, aiding in disaster preparedness and response.

AI and machine learning are becoming central to climate research. Google's DeepMind worked with the UK Met Office to improve short-term rainfall forecasts using an AI model trained on radar data. When tested by more than 50 expert meteorologists, the system was rated more accurate and useful than traditional methods in nearly 90 percent of cases. This kind of short-term forecasting, known as nowcasting, can help provide earlier warnings for severe weather.

Supercomputing remains vital for climate modeling, especially at institutions like the UK Met Office and the U.S. Department of Energy. These high-performance systems simulate complex climate scenarios, but even the most advanced supercomputers face obstacles in handling the intricate, interconnected systems that drive climate. Quantum computing could offer an alternative approach by processing multiple interdependent variables at once. This capability would enable quantum computers to manage the large datasets behind climate predictions more efficiently, allowing for deeper insights.

With quantum-enhanced climate models, researchers could simulate multiple environmental factors at the same time. This includes temperature changes, rainfall patterns, and extreme weather events. IBM's Quantum Network, in collaboration with research institutions, is working on algorithms that capture the complex interactions between atmospheric and oceanic conditions. This approach offers new ways for climate scientists to understand the environmental factors that influence global change.

Quantum technology could also improve predictions for extreme events like hurricanes, wildfires, and floods, where precise forecasting is essential. Researchers at **NASA's Quantum Artificial Intelligence Laboratory (QuAIL)**, in partnership with D-Wave, are developing algorithms to improve forecasting accuracy. These advancements could provide emergency responders with more reliable and timely information, which is critical for protecting vulnerable communities.

Efforts to build climate resilience are underway, with IBM using quantum algorithms to study interactions among atmospheric layers, ocean currents, and environmental pollutants. By identifying subtle patterns that traditional models might overlook, quantum-enhanced simulations could help researchers design more effective strategies for dealing with climate issues. This shift could lead to a preventive approach in climate science, equipping scientists and policymakers with tools to better manage climate impacts.

Besides renewables, next-generation nuclear power is a promising path to lower carbon emissions. Small modular reactors (SMRs) and other advanced nuclear designs address issues like safety, waste management, and scalability. SMRs are compact and versatile, designed to be safer and easier to set up than traditional nuclear plants. They can operate in remote locations or integrate with renewable energy grids, providing consistent and reliable power.

Firms such as NuScale in the U.S. and Rolls-Royce in the U.K. are leading in SMR technology, with some models expected to be commercially available by the 2030s.

Other nuclear innovations, such as molten salt and fast reactors, are focused on safety and efficiency. Molten salt reactors use liquid salt as both a coolant and a fuel carrier, allowing them to operate at lower pressures while maintaining high temperatures. This design enhances safety by reducing the risk of high-pressure failures. TerraPower, with backing from Bill Gates, is developing molten salt reactors that self-regulate, further minimizing the risks often associated with nuclear energy. Fast reactors recycle spent fuel, cutting down on nuclear waste while maximizing energy output from available resources, lowering the environmental impact of nuclear power.

Quantum computing could also support nuclear research by allowing for detailed simulations of materials that can endure extreme radiation and temperatures; a necessity for building durable reactors. Quantum simulations could aid fusion research as well, potentially helping scientists make strides toward achieving sustained nuclear fusion, which could be a clean, nearly limitless energy source.

Quantum computing shows potential in renewable energy and sustainability too. In renewable energy grids, optimization is crucial for integrating solar, wind, and other sources. Quantum computers can handle large datasets on weather patterns, storage capacities, and demand fluctuations, enabling real-time adjustments to improve grid efficiency. Google's Quantum AI team is working with energy providers to develop quantum algorithms that stabilize grids, making renewable sources more reliable.

Battery and energy storage technology are essential for electric vehicles (EVs) and large-scale renewable systems. Volkswagen's quantum research team, working with quantum tech partners, is exploring new materials for longer-lasting batteries, potentially extending EV range and making large-scale energy storage more effective.

In renewable energy material discovery, the focus is on improving efficiency and cutting costs for technologies like solar cells and wind turbines. Perovskite materials, with their unique crystal structure, efficiently absorb light, offering opportunities for solar energy. Unlike traditional silicon panels, perovskite solar cells can be made at lower temperatures and applied to flexible surfaces, potentially creating lightweight and adaptable solar solutions. Quantum startup Xanadu is using quantum simulations to enhance perovskite materials, aiming for solar cells that perform well in low light or extreme temperatures.

Carbon capture and sequestration (CCS) is crucial for cutting CO_2 emissions. CCS captures carbon dioxide before it enters the atmosphere, storing it underground or repurposing it for industrial use. Quantum computing could speed up the discovery of materials that absorb and store carbon more effectively, making CCS more efficient and affordable. At the UK's National Quantum Technology Hub, researchers are developing quantum-enhanced CCS methods. By simulating molecular interactions between CO_2 and various materials, quantum algorithms can help identify compounds that improve absorption and storage rates, making CCS scalable. This research aims to create CCS technologies that help industries lower their carbon footprints and meet global emission reduction targets.

Hydrogen fuel cells offer another clean energy solution, especially for transportation. Quantum computing could help identify materials that increase fuel cell efficiency, reducing dependence on expensive catalysts like platinum. **Airbus**, collaborating with quantum researchers, is working to develop more efficient hydrogen fuel cells, bringing hydrogen-powered aviation closer to reality.

Together, these advances underscore quantum computing's potential to drive sustainability, building a foundation for a cleaner, more efficient future. In climate science, combining AI with quantum computing could reform environmental modeling by merging predictive tools with real-time data analysis. In data preprocessing, AI handles large climate datasets, identifying trends for quantum systems to simulate with precision. By preparing the data, AI allows quantum computers to focus on crucial scenarios, accelerating insights into climate patterns.

For renewable energy infrastructure, AI and quantum computing together support grid stability and efficiency by forecasting shifts in supply and demand based on weather and usage patterns. This synergy enhances grid reliability, reduces dependence on fossil fuels, and cuts emissions.

Quantum computing in finance and security

Integrating quantum computing into finance and security brings both significant opportunities and serious challenges. This technology has the potential to change how we manage financial assets, evaluate risks, and protect sensitive information. Its ability to challenge current encryption methods highlights the need for forward-thinking solutions to safeguard digital systems, including blockchain networks. In this chapter, we'll examine how to balance the benefits of quantum computing with its risks, focusing on its role in portfolio optimization, fraud detection, secure communications, and advancements in blockchain technology.

Finance and optimization

What if financial markets could analyze risks as easily as counting coins, optimize portfolios in the blink of an eye, and detect fraud before it happens? Quantum computing could change the financial world, enabling faster, smarter, and more secure decisions.

The financial sector is a major component of the global economy, valued at over $20 trillion. It includes banking, investment management, insurance, and more, supporting industries, innovation, and personal livelihoods. Financial institutions manage enormous flows of capital, assess risks, and refine investments to keep up with shifting markets. Decision-making in finance relies heavily on analyzing intricate data quickly, adjusting to factors like economic indicators, asset performance, social trends, and global events.

Quantum computing offers new opportunities for the financial sector, providing enhanced tools for optimization, risk assessment, and fraud detection by processing large datasets in parallel. Unlike traditional computers, which examine one variable at a time, quantum computers can handle multiple variables simultaneously. This ability could reduce analysis time from days to mere seconds, enabling financial firms to respond to market shifts at unprecedented speeds.

Investment banks and hedge funds are at the forefront of this shift. Firms such as Goldman Sachs, JPMorgan Chase, and Citadel are heavily invested in quantum research, focusing on improving trading strategies, optimizing portfolios, and refining risk management through faster, more accurate modeling. Similarly, asset managers such as BlackRock and Vanguard are exploring quantum computing to analyze a range of asset classes at once, accelerating decision-making in fast-paced markets.

Technology companies and quantum startups play a critical role in advancing quantum solutions for finance. Firms such as Google and IBM, along with quantum-specialized companies such as Rigetti and D-Wave, work closely with financial institutions to develop quantum algorithms for advanced data processing, fraud detection, and predictive market analysis. Meanwhile, regulatory bodies such as the U.S. Securities and Exchange Commission (SEC), the European Central Bank (ECB), and other global financial authorities provide essential oversight. As quantum computing integrates further into finance, these regulators may need to adapt their frameworks to address the unique risks and benefits that quantum technology brings to the financial landscape.

Several core challenges in finance could be addressed by quantum computing and AI. Portfolio optimization, a process where financial institutions balance returns, risks, and regulatory needs spanning thousands of assets, is one key area. Traditional optimization methods can be slow, delaying responses to sudden market changes. Quantum computing could make real-time, data-driven decisions possible, vastly speeding up the process.

Risk assessment is another area where quantum systems may prove invaluable. Financial risk modeling requires examining countless interconnected risk factors, especially during market volatility. Quantum computers can analyze these connections simultaneously, revealing vulnerabilities that traditional systems might miss. For instance, JPMorgan Chase has invested in quantum algorithms designed to improve risk analysis in derivatives trading, helping traders manage exposure in unpredictable markets.

Fraud detection is a top priority in an increasingly digital and fast-paced financial landscape. As transaction volumes grow, so does the challenge of identifying fraudulent activities without delaying legitimate transactions. Quantum computing's parallel processing capabilities make it well-suited for real-time analysis of transaction patterns, quickly identifying anomalies. A common issue in fraud detection systems today is "false positives", alerts triggered by innocent actions that appear suspicious. During COVID-19, people may recall "false positives" in testing, where results incorrectly showed infection. In finance, false positives waste resources and delay responses by flagging routine transactions as potential fraud. Quantum systems are better able to distinguish actual threats from innocent patterns, potentially reducing these costly errors. Rigetti Computing, for example, has partnered with financial institutions to develop quantum algorithms that detect fraud by analyzing transaction patterns more accurately and reliably.

Quantum technology could also simplify regulatory compliance by processing large amounts of data required for audits and transaction screenings more efficiently. Financial institutions such as JPMorgan Chase and HSBC have established dedicated quantum research teams to develop applications in areas like risk modeling and compliance. Additionally, firms like Multiverse Computing are collaborating with banks including BBVA and

Crédit Agricole CIB to apply quantum algorithms for tasks such as fraud detection and regulatory reporting. These efforts aim to enhance transparency in reporting and auditing, thereby helping to maintain trust in financial markets.

Quantum computing could play a valuable role in **high-frequency trading (HFT)** and algorithmic trading, enabling orders to be executed in milliseconds. Many firms rely on these methods to make fast trades. Quantum computing could further refine HFT by speeding up data processing and optimizing algorithms, offering firms a competitive edge in real-time trading. As data continues to grow, financial institutions are working to analyze extensive datasets, from transaction records to market sentiment, to make better-informed decisions. Quantum computing's ability to handle multiple data points at once could push analytics beyond current limits, revealing insights that classical systems might struggle to capture.

Several companies are already exploring quantum computing's potential to improve financial processes. D-Wave's quantum annealers, tested with OTI Lumionics for portfolio optimization, have shown potential in balancing returns and risks across diverse asset classes. Goldman Sachs, in partnership with IBM, is developing quantum algorithms to assess risks in derivatives faster than traditional systems, offering better tools for managing market exposure. JPMorgan Chase's work with IBM focuses on using quantum algorithms to improve option pricing, reduce calculation times, and enable quicker decisions.

Standard Chartered has teamed up with quantum firms to test algorithms for capital allocation, to distribute resources more efficiently, and to adopt swiftly to regulatory demands. Meanwhile, **Volkswagen's Quantum Lab** is researching quantum-enhanced models for predictive trading, examining market variable correlations for improved accuracy in forecasting.

These ongoing projects underscore quantum computing's growing role in finance, with each project enhancing processes vital to the industry, from portfolio management to market prediction and risk assessment.

Looking to the future, quantum computing is expected to be beneficial for addressing long-standing challenges in finance, and enabling new solutions in optimization, risk management, and security. Quantum computers can process multiple datasets simultaneously, delivering deeper insights into portfolio optimization. Financial institutions could analyze thousands of assets in real-time, balancing potential returns with market risks as conditions develop. Goldman Sachs, for instance, is researching quantum algorithms that may offer more precise portfolio management, potentially reducing risk while maximizing returns.

Quantum technology could also strengthen market stability by helping financial institutions make data-driven decisions during times of volatility, reducing the likelihood of extreme market shifts. Quantum-enhanced analysis allows institutions to detect early signs of stress in the markets, enabling proactive responses. This added stability benefits institutional investors and contributes to a more resilient global financial system.

As quantum technology progresses, it has the potential to reshape finance by enabling more tailored financial products and adaptable market structures. Combined with AI, quantum computing can generate insights that classical systems struggle to produce quickly enough.

Cryptography and cybersecurity

As quantum computers grow more powerful, they may outpace today's encryption methods, forcing a shift to quantum-safe systems that safeguard everything from online banking to government secrets. Quantum technology itself may be the key to securing the digital future.

As the digital world grows, cybersecurity has become essential for protecting sensitive information, securing online communication, and safeguarding privacy. The cryptography industry, worth billions of dollars, is critical for ensuring security in everything from personal banking to international communications. However, as more interactions take place online, the risk of breaches has increased. Traditional encryption techniques, like **RSA** and **Elliptic Curve Cryptography** (**ECC**), rely on mathematical puzzles that would take classical computers thousands of years to solve. While these methods are secure by today's standards, the rapid development of quantum computing could soon make current encryption methods vulnerable. This looming risk has led to an urgent need for "quantum-safe" solutions.

Major technology leaders like IBM, Google, and quantum-focused companies such as D-Wave and Rigetti, alongside cybersecurity firms like RSA Security and Symantec, are addressing this challenge. Organizations such as the National Institute of Standards and Technology (NIST) are leading efforts to create **post-quantum cryptography** (**PQC**) standards to protect data in a quantum-powered future.

Quantum computing introduces a new level of urgency for cybersecurity, especially regarding encryption. To understand why, consider RSA encryption, one of the most widely used encryption methods today. RSA secures data by using a pair of keys: a public key for encrypting data and a private key for decrypting it. Nearly all applications currently rely on RSA in some form, securing everything from online banking and email to digital signatures and web browsing. RSA is also used in countless other areas we encounter every day, like verifying the identity of websites, protecting credit card information during online shopping, and securing transactions at ATMs. It even plays a role in mobile apps, medical record systems, and connected devices, such as smart home assistants. Essentially, RSA safeguards sensitive information in countless ways that are fundamental to modern digital life.

The security of RSA relies on the difficulty of factoring a large number, typically the product of two prime numbers. This is a challenging task for classical computers, making RSA secure for now. However, quantum computing changes this equation with an algorithm known as Shor's algorithm, which is specifically designed to efficiently factor large numbers. Shor's algorithm works by taking advantage of quantum mechanics to handle many calculations simultaneously, which is a departure from how classical computers process information step-by-step.

In simple terms, Shor's algorithm allows a quantum computer to quickly find the factors of a large number by trying multiple possibilities at once, rather than one at a time, as a classical computer would. This parallel processing power dramatically reduces the time needed to find factors, allowing quantum computers to break down problems that classical computers would take thousands of years to solve.

If you remember the example of folding a piece of paper 42 times to reach the moon, this illustrates exponential growth. Each fold doubles the paper's thickness, and this doubling accumulates so rapidly that, after only 42 folds, the thickness would reach a distance comparable to that from Earth to the moon. This example shows how exponential growth can produce enormous results in surprisingly few steps. Similarly, quantum computing could handle factoring problems exponentially faster than classical computers. For instance, RSA-2048 encryption, which relies on the difficulty of factoring large numbers, would require roughly 4,000 to 6,000 error-corrected qubits to break; a capability quantum computers don't yet have. But once quantum technology reaches this threshold, Shor's algorithm could allow sensitive data to be decrypted in hours, posing a significant threat to everything from government information to private transactions.

To counter this, researchers are developing quantum-safe encryption algorithms that can resist both quantum and classical attacks. One promising method is lattice-based cryptography, which works like navigating a complex 3D maze to hide information. Data is embedded within a lattice; a multidimensional grid structure that would require massive computing power to navigate and decode, even for quantum computers. The strength of lattice-based cryptography lies in its intricate "grid" of data points, making it extremely hard to pinpoint any specific data within it without the correct key. Picture data spread across countless intersections in a web of pathways; without the precise directions, locating a particular piece of information becomes nearly impossible. NIST is actively researching lattice-based cryptography, collaborating with IBM to promote this approach.

Adding another layer of security is **quantum key distribution (QKD)**, a system that changes how encryption keys (the "passwords" for securing data) are shared. Unlike classical methods, which involve sending keys over channels that could be intercepted, QKD uses the principles of quantum mechanics (or rather **quantum cryptography**) to make any eavesdropping attempts immediately detectable. Here's how it works: when encryption keys are transmitted through QKD, they are sent in quantum states that will alter if they're observed or tampered with, alerting the intended receiver of any interception. This method has already been tested successfully. For instance, China's **Micius satellite** showed QKD by securely transmitting data between Beijing and Vienna, proving its effectiveness in protecting sensitive communication. Quantinuum, among others, is exploring how QKD can enhance data security in various areas.

On the topic of Micius, this satellite didn't just showcase secure communication through QKD; it also achieved a breakthrough in quantum teleportation, a concept that sounds straight out of science fiction. The popular sci-fi series Star Trek famously introduced the "transporter" device, allowing characters to be instantly "beamed" from one place to another, sparking a fascination with teleportation. While Star Trek's teleportation involved moving physical matter, quantum teleportation works differently. Instead of moving objects or people, it transfers the quantum state of one particle to another distant particle using quantum entanglement, a process that enables a replica of the original particle's state to be recreated far away.

Quantum teleportation with Micius was used to transfer quantum states of photons between locations, demonstrating the potential for securely transmitting quantum information over great distances. Although it doesn't involve physical objects like in Star Trek, this method has significant implications for secure communication, as it could enable instant, tamper-proof data transfer in future quantum networks. For now, quantum teleportation is limited to information transfer and remains a complex technical feat, but it highlights just how quickly quantum communication is advancing. By exploring these quantum ideas, both scientists and science fiction have broadened our view of what might one day be achievable, turning what once seemed like fantasy into actual progress in quantum mechanics.

The ability of quantum computing to analyze large datasets rapidly also brings benefits for threat detection. IBM and Google are working on quantum-based simulations for cybersecurity, aiming to identify potential vulnerabilities before attackers can exploit them. By leveraging these quantum-enhanced models, they aim to build cybersecurity systems that stay ahead of growing threats.

This shift toward quantum-safe encryption and real-time security systems also aligns with data protection regulations, such as the GDPR (General Data Protection Regulation) in the European Union, which sets strict rules for data privacy and security. As more data is processed and stored digitally, quantum-safe encryption methods could play a critical role in protecting personal information from future threats. Compliance with standards like GDPR may soon require businesses to adopt encryption that withstands both quantum and classical attacks, as regulators anticipate the impact of quantum advancements on data privacy.

Quantum computing and AI are paving the way for future cybersecurity systems. With quantum-safe encryption, QKD protocols, and predictive threat models, future networks could provide proactive protection for sensitive data. This shift could help secure essential infrastructures such as financial networks, and government services, building a digital landscape that can withstand quantum-based threats. Quantinuum's work with healthcare providers to protect patient data, for example, shows the potential of quantum technology to enhance data privacy.

Blockchain

*Picture a **blockchain** system that develops with quantum technology, resistant to future threats while unlocking efficiencies we can barely dream of today. Quantum computing may rewrite the rules of decentralized systems, making them faster, stronger, and more secure.*

Blockchain has advanced rapidly since Bitcoin's introduction, becoming a central technology in areas like finance, supply chains, and digital security. It operates through a decentralized, tamper-resistant structure that verifies and records transactions securely, building trust in value transfers, asset management, and data protection.

The origins of blockchain technology trace back to 2008 with the introduction of Bitcoin by the anonymous **Satoshi Nakamoto**. Nakamoto's invention marked the start of a system that bypasses traditional middlemen, allowing secure, peer-to-peer transactions. When Bitcoin launched in 2009, it laid the groundwork for blockchain technology to expand beyond cryptocurrency into many other fields.

Today, blockchain powers a wide range of applications, from cryptocurrency to global supply chains. It's being developed by major players like IBM, Google, and cybersecurity firms such as RSA Security and Symantec, along with blockchain specialists like D-Wave and Rigetti. Meanwhile, organizations like the National Institute of Standards and Technology (NIST) are setting security standards as blockchain becomes more integrated into the digital landscape.

A blockchain can be described as a *digital ledger*, but instead of being kept in a single location, it's spread across many computers. Each transaction is recorded in a block, and these blocks are linked in a chain. Once a block is added to the chain, it's incredibly difficult to change, ensuring the integrity of the information. This distributed and secure nature of blockchain makes it a reliable and transparent system for recording transactions.

When a transaction occurs, it's verified by a network of participants who use a consensus mechanism. Common mechanisms include Proof of Work (PoW) and Proof of Stake (PoS). In PoW, participants (often called miners) compete to solve complex mathematical puzzles, validating transactions and creating new blocks in the process. In PoS, participants validate transactions based on the number of coins they hold, reducing the computational intensity compared to PoW. By removing centralized control, blockchain creates a level of security and transparency that traditional databases lack, with all records visible to network participants. Once added to the chain, data is permanently stored and cannot be altered, which makes blockchain useful for records that require transparency and reliability, such as financial transactions or supply chain data.

Quantum computing poses a significant future risk to blockchain encryption. Quantum computers can run algorithms, like Shor's, that might break encryption protocols such as RSA and Elliptic Curve Cryptography (ECC) at much faster speeds than classical computers. Recognizing this potential risk, researchers are developing "quantum-safe" encryption, or post-quantum cryptographic (PQC) algorithms, which are being tested and standardized by organizations like NIST.

Beyond addressing security, quantum computing could also enhance blockchain's efficiency. Quantum computers' ability to handle large data sets in parallel could make consensus mechanisms more efficient. For instance, PoS could benefit from true randomness introduced by quantum processes, making the selection of validating nodes more secure and less predictable.

Quantum hash functions are a cutting-edge technology that could significantly enhance the security of blockchains. In simple terms, hash functions create unique digital fingerprints for data. Think of them as a unique code generated for each transaction. Currently, these codes are very difficult to reverse-engineer, making it nearly impossible to alter past transactions. Quantum hash functions would take this security to the next level, making it even harder for malicious actors to tamper with the blockchain.

Research efforts are underway to protect blockchain against quantum risks while improving its performance. IBM, working closely with NIST, leads studies in quantum-safe cryptography, particularly lattice-based techniques, which are resistant to quantum attacks. The Ethereum Foundation is also preparing for quantum security, exploring methods to strengthen its PoS blockchain, and D-Wave's quantum annealing systems are being tested to improve blockchain's efficiency by solving complex optimization challenges.

The convergence of quantum computing and blockchain presents both risks and opportunities. While quantum computing could undermine some existing protections, it also offers new possibilities for securing and enhancing blockchain. Proactive development of quantum-resistant encryption and improved consensus processes will help prepare blockchain to thrive in a quantum-powered digital landscape, creating a future where blockchain and quantum technology complement each other to establish a more secure, efficient infrastructure.

Quantum computing for infrastructure and planning

The systems that define our modern world, from transportation networks and energy grids to urban environments and agriculture, stand to benefit significantly from quantum computing. In this chapter, we'll look at how this technology can optimize the interconnected systems that support our infrastructure and help plan sustainable, adaptable communities. By applying quantum computing's unique capabilities, we can achieve greater efficiency, flexibility, and environmental responsibility, creating a future where our built environments and resource management are guided by precision and informed decision-making.

Logistics sector

Picture this: a world where every package arrives precisely when expected, routes adapt instantly to traffic or weather, and supply chains run smoothly, even on the busiest days. Quantum computing could turn this vision into reality, creating a logistics network that operates with unmatched efficiency and reliability.

The logistics sector, spanning freight, warehousing, supply chain management, and last-mile delivery, is a cornerstone of the global economy. With a market worth over $5 trillion, logistics powers the movement of goods worldwide, impacting trade, commerce, and daily life. As customer expectations rise, companies in logistics must improve operations, speed up deliveries, and lower their environmental impact. Although once reliant on manual work and basic automation, the industry now benefits from rapid advances in technology, with AI, machine learning, and quantum computing leading the way.

Historically, logistics focused on physical work and local distribution. With globalization and the rise of e-commerce, it has evolved into a highly data-driven operation. Companies now depend on real-time information to adapt to market shifts, consumer demand, and global disruptions such as pandemics and supply chain delays. Industry leaders like UPS, FedEx, DHL, and Amazon use advanced technologies to optimize delivery and improve efficiency.

Recent research suggests that quantum computing could help solve some of logistics' most difficult problems, such as route optimization and complex supply chain planning. For example, DHL has published white papers exploring how quantum computing could improve delivery route planning and warehouse layout design. Volkswagen has partnered with D-Wave to test quantum algorithms for traffic flow optimization in cities like Barcelona and Beijing. Their early results showed that quantum computing could create more efficient routing for vehicle fleets, reducing congestion and improving fuel efficiency.

Other companies, such as Zapata Computing and Classiq, have also announced collaborations with logistics providers to explore supply chain modeling and optimization using quantum algorithms. These efforts reflect growing interest in applying quantum tools to challenges where classical systems struggle to keep up.

One of the central problems in logistics is route optimization, often illustrated by the Traveling Salesman Problem (TSP). In TSP, the challenge is to find the shortest possible route that allows a delivery driver (the "salesman") to visit a set of locations and return to the starting point. With only a few stops, finding the best route is straightforward, but as the number of locations grows, the potential routes multiply dramatically. For example, with 20 stops, there are about 2.4 million possible routes, and with 30 stops, the number jumps to around 30 billion. This explosion in potential routes makes it almost impossible for traditional computers to process every option efficiently.

Quantum computing offers an advantage here because it can evaluate multiple possibilities at once. Quantum systems approach the TSP by testing a large number of routes in parallel, which allows logistics companies to find optimal or near-optimal routes far faster than classical computers. This means companies can save on fuel, reduce delivery times, and cut emissions, creating a more efficient and eco-friendly operation. By solving TSP more effectively, quantum computing enables logistics firms to handle complex scenarios that would otherwise be too slow or costly to manage with traditional systems.

Leading logistics companies, including UPS, FedEx, DHL, and Amazon Logistics, are setting new standards in route optimization, delivery systems, and warehouse management. Their goal is to incorporate cutting-edge technology that simplifies deliveries, reduces costs, and improves operational efficiency. Freight and supply chain management giants like Maersk and DB Schenker coordinate the flow of goods across borders, managing diverse logistics needs while balancing cost and efficiency. Tech giants and quantum startups like IBM, Google, D-Wave, and Rigetti have partnered with logistics firms to explore quantum solutions for real-time route adjustments, dynamic supply chain management, and greater operational efficiency. Regulatory bodies and environmental advocates, such as the Department of Transportation (DOT), play essential roles in setting and enforcing sustainability standards, ensuring the industry progresses in an eco-friendly direction.

The logistics industry faces many hurdles, with route optimization standing out as a core challenge. As delivery volumes increase, companies must identify the most efficient paths to save fuel and time. However, as the number of stops and potential routes grows, traditional systems struggle to process all options efficiently. Additionally, the rise of electric self-driving trucks will change logistics dramatically. Organizations such as Tesla and Waymo are developing autonomous trucks that operate on electric power, allowing for near-continuous operation without human limits like rest breaks. Quantum computing could further optimize these fleets by calculating the most efficient routes and charging schedules in real-time, ensuring that trucks run smoothly while lowering energy use and emissions.

Another area where quantum technology could provide value is predictive maintenance. AI and Internet of Things (IoT) sensors already allow companies to track vehicle performance and predict maintenance needs before issues arise. Quantum computing could improve this process by analyzing significant amounts of sensor data from electric and autonomous vehicles to detect subtle patterns that show when repairs are needed. This proactive approach reduces downtime, minimizes repair costs, and extends the lifespan of both vehicles and machinery.

Warehouse automation is also advancing with the help of AI-driven robotics. Companies like Amazon and Ocado have introduced robotic systems that sort, pack, and manage inventory with impressive speed and accuracy. Quantum algorithms could play a future role here by synchronizing robotic fleets in real time, optimizing their tasks to handle shifting demand and reduce operational costs. This creates highly efficient warehouse environments that can adapt instantly to changing needs.

However, as these systems become more advanced, they also raise important questions about the future of work. Many warehouse and logistics jobs that are currently handled by people may eventually be replaced by machines. While automation can improve safety and efficiency, it also risks displacing large segments of the workforce, particularly in roles that have long provided stable employment. As the technology progresses, society will need to consider how to balance innovation with job security and economic inclusion.

In recent years, logistics companies have heavily invested in technology to meet growing consumer demands for faster deliveries while managing higher operational costs. AI and machine learning are already streamlining tasks like warehouse management and demand forecasting. Now, the industry is looking toward quantum computing for the next breakthrough, as quantum algorithms hold the potential to reduce inefficiencies such as fuel waste and idle labor that account for 10-20% of logistics costs. According to Boston Consulting Group, quantum technology could help major logistics firms save billions each year.

As quantum technology progresses, logistics could see hyper-efficient, low-carbon supply chains. Future applications might include predictive logistics for peak times, with AI and quantum working together to forecast demand spikes during holidays or sales events. This enables logistics firms to adjust resources and routes in advance, ensuring timely deliveries during periods of high demand. Quantum computing could also enhance last-mile delivery, especially in cities where traffic congestion is common. Organizations such as Amazon are already exploring quantum optimization techniques to streamline urban delivery routes and improve efficiency, aligning sustainability with business needs.

In addition, quantum technology could improve supply chain resilience. By rapidly adapting to disruptions like natural disasters, port closures, or supply shortages, quantum solutions help ensure goods reach their destinations without delay.

Urban planning and smart cities

Picture a city where energy grids balance themselves, traffic flows without congestion, and emergency responses are coordinated in seconds. Quantum technology could pave the way for smarter, more sustainable cities that adapt effortlessly to the needs of their residents.

Urban planning and smart city initiatives are vital for making cities more efficient, sustainable, and livable, especially as urban populations grow. Rapid urbanization puts pressure on infrastructure, resources, and services, calling for innovative solutions. Smart cities use advanced technologies like the IoT, AI, and big data analytics, to improve city functions, such as transportation, energy management, water distribution, waste management, and emergency response. Quantum computing, as it advances, will add valuable support for managing these intricate systems while minimizing environmental impact.

Worldwide, several major cities are leading smart city development. In China, the Smart City Initiative includes over 500 pilot projects with ambitious goals to integrate technology into urban life. One highlight is **Xiong'an New Area**, a high-tech, eco-friendly city in progress, about 100 kilometers southwest of Beijing and spanning 1,770 square kilometers (an area roughly the size of Chicago). Established in 2017, Xiong'an aims to reduce Beijing's overpopulation while promoting sustainable development, green technology, and smart infrastructure. Key functions are expected to be operational by 2035, with full completion by 2050. Focusing on integrating IoT and AI, Xiong'an collects real-time data on air quality, traffic, and other urban metrics to efficiently manage resources and reduce emissions. Its energy system, for example, prioritizes renewable sources like solar and wind, using AI to distribute energy across the grid.

As quantum technology matures, Xiong'an plans to integrate quantum-enhanced solutions to improve urban management. Quantum computing could provide predictive models for energy distribution, balancing the load on its grid for greater efficiency with lower environmental impact. Quantum key distribution (QKD) could secure the city's digital networks, protecting data across its IoT framework. For traffic management, quantum simulations could analyze real-time data to adjust routes and prevent congestion, making city movement smoother. Xiong'an stands as a model for future smart cities worldwide, blending green technology with advanced urban planning to support China's position in the global quantum race.

Singapore's Smart Nation Initiative has also set a global benchmark in urban technology. By utilizing data analytics, AI, and IoT, Singapore optimizes public transport, energy use, and public safety. In Dubai, smart city efforts include plans to incorporate quantum computing for predictive urban planning and energy efficiency, further highlighting the global shift towards data-driven urban management.

Besides these city-led projects, technology companies such as IBM, Siemens, and Microsoft are contributing to smart city development by exploring how quantum computing and AI can be combined to support traffic optimization, energy use, and emergency response. Research institutions, including MIT and **Los Alamos National**

Laboratory, are also studying how quantum solutions could improve disaster preparedness and help plan resilient urban infrastructure.

To build efficient, sustainable cities, resource management is critical. With urban expansion, balancing the use of resources like water, energy, and waste with environmental goals becomes increasingly challenging. Effective resource management helps reduce urban carbon footprints and adapts cities to climate-related pressures.

Traffic congestion, which reduces productivity and worsens air quality, is another pressing issue. Despite advances in traffic systems, managing large-scale, real-time systems remains an intricate task. The huge amounts of data produced by smart city sensors, cameras, and IoT devices require swift and secure processing to maintain public safety and privacy.

Quantum computing could solve many of these urban challenges by analyzing large datasets quickly and simulating different scenarios at once. This capacity for real-time analysis could help cities fine-tune systems for traffic, energy use, and waste reduction. For instance, Volkswagen's project on quantum computing in traffic management aims to reduce urban travel times, cut emissions, and enhance public transportation efficiency.

In energy management, quantum computing can help cities balance supply and demand more efficiently, especially as more renewable sources enter the grid. In the Netherlands, energy companies are exploring quantum technology to optimize grids, making them more reliable and capable of prioritizing renewable energy. With predictive models, quantum systems could help cities adjust energy use in real-time, reducing reliance on fossil fuels and lowering environmental impacts.

Quantum computing could provide advantages for improving water and waste management. By predicting water consumption patterns, optimizing storage, and improving distribution, cities can ensure sustainable water use. Quantum simulations could also streamline waste management by refining collection routes and recycling processes, offering cost-effective solutions to waste disposal while minimizing environmental harm.

In emergency response and disaster preparedness, quantum computing could model disaster scenarios to help cities plan for natural emergencies like earthquakes and floods. Quantum algorithms can calculate evacuation routes, allocate resources, and predict the effects of various strategies. Collaborations between research centers, such as Los Alamos National Laboratory and Fujitsu, already explore quantum-based disaster simulations. In real-time crises, quantum systems could adjust evacuation plans based on traffic, road damage, or building conditions, ensuring efficient response during emergencies.

As quantum technology advances, it will enable cities to be more adaptable and responsive to residents' needs. By combining AI's analytical strengths with quantum computing's ability to process extensive data rapidly, cities can create "digital urban twins"; virtual replicas that simulate the outcomes of different policies and projects. **IBM's Urban Twin project**, for example, combines quantum and AI to develop predictive models, allowing planners to make better decisions on zoning, infrastructure, and policy without relying on trial and error.

Quantum technology will also benefit green urban spaces by simulating the environmental effects of different designs, helping cities develop parks, green roofs, and other sustainable features that improve air quality, reduce urban heat, and contribute to overall resilience.

Quantum computing's role in urban planning will be key to shaping sustainable, efficient cities. By managing resources effectively, improving transportation, and reducing environmental impact, quantum solutions can help cities prepare for the challenges of population growth and climate change. Through partnerships among governments, tech companies, and research institutions, quantum technology will support the development of cities that are more efficient, adaptable, and resilient for future generations.

Precision agriculture

Imagine a farm where every crop gets exactly what it needs, no more, no less. Optimized by quantum-powered systems that predict the weather, manage resources, and increase yields. Quantum computing could help feed the world while protecting the planet.

Precision agriculture is reshaping farming by using advanced technology to improve efficiency, boost productivity, and support sustainability. This approach addresses urgent challenges like climate change, limited resources, and increasing global food demand. Unlike traditional farming, which applies the same methods across large fields, precision agriculture customizes techniques to address the specific needs of different areas within the same farm. By targeting resources this way, farmers can increase yields, conserve resources, and lower environmental impacts. Technologies such as AI-driven data analysis, IoT sensors, satellite imagery, and quantum computing each play a role in helping farmers make better decisions and operate more effectively.

Many companies are already advancing these practices. For instance, **John Deere** uses **See & Spray** technology, which applies AI to identify crops and weeds, reducing the need for pesticides. Bayer Crop Science's Climate FieldView platform monitors crop health, optimizing inputs to increase yields, and is exploring how quantum computing might improve crop growth forecasts and disease management. Microsoft Azure Quantum, in collaboration with partners, is investigating quantum applications that could enhance agriculture by refining crop yield predictions, optimizing resource management, and strengthening supply chains. Similarly, startups like Xanadu use quantum algorithms to improve energy use and forecast agricultural needs through quantum simulations.

Despite its potential, precision agriculture faces certain obstacles. Climate variability including droughts and floods, can significantly impact crop yields. The rising demand for food adds pressure on limited resources, such as water and fertile land, making efficient resource management essential. Traditional farming practices also contribute to environmental challenges like pesticide runoff and soil degradation. Precision agriculture aims to reduce these effects, but achieving sustainability will require ongoing technological progress.

With the immense amount of data collected from sensors, satellites, and weather reports, efficient data processing becomes crucial. This is where quantum computing has real potential. By speeding up simulations and calculations, quantum computing can help process complex datasets faster than traditional systems, enabling simulations that consider multiple variables at once. This capability can be vital for improving crop yields, managing resources, and reducing environmental impacts.

For example, quantum computing can simulate real-time interactions between soil conditions, weather, and irrigation, allowing farmers to make the most of resources like water, fertilizers, and pesticides. AI helps analyze this data to make useful predictions, while quantum computing accelerates simulations, providing insights much faster than classical systems can. IBM's research in fields like carbon capture and renewable energy also highlights how quantum computing can support sustainable practices and resource efficiency, with potential benefits for agriculture, including reduced waste and lower energy use.

Quantum computing also supports advancements in materials science that directly benefit farming. Simulating properties at the atomic level helps create better equipment, vehicles, and energy-efficient systems, all of which contribute to more sustainable agricultural practices. In energy storage, for instance, quantum simulations are being used to improve battery technology, which could lead to more efficient energy use in farming equipment. Toyota's efforts to enhance energy storage for electric vehicles through quantum simulations could bring similar improvements to farming technology, making machinery more efficient and reducing environmental impact.

The future of quantum-powered precision agriculture envisions systems that respond to environmental changes in real-time. With data from drones, satellites, and sensors, quantum-AI platforms could adjust planting, irrigation, and harvesting strategies based on factors like soil nutrients, crop health, and even market demand. Such adaptive systems would allow farmers to increase yields while reducing waste. By predicting the best times for planting and harvesting, farmers could boost productivity and minimize food loss. AI and quantum computing hybrids might also provide ongoing crop health monitoring, adjusting practices based on up-to-date information.

Google's work with quantum sensing technology is another step forward in precision agriculture. Unlike traditional precision agriculture, which relies on data from GPS, drones, and IoT devices, quantum sensing introduces an unprecedented level of sensitivity, capable of detecting subtle changes in environmental conditions. Google's quantum sensors, for example, collect real-time data on soil composition, nutrients, and moisture with exceptional precision. This allows farmers to spot slight changes in crop health, soil conditions, and environmental stress that conventional sensors might miss. With such accurate and timely data, farmers can take preventive actions that reduce crop loss, improve yields, and increase efficiency.

Quantum sensing technology presents opportunities for resource conservation. By providing precise data on soil nutrients, quantum sensors help farmers apply fertilizers accurately, minimizing waste, lowering costs, and reducing the environmental impact of over-fertilization. Quantum sensing also enables better water management: exact soil moisture readings allow for optimized irrigation schedules that save water while supporting crop health; a significant advantage in areas facing water shortages. Quantum sensing aids climate adaptation by closely monitoring environmental factors, helping farmers prepare for extreme weather and adjust their practices to changing conditions. Although quantum sensing technology is currently costly, its potential to drive significant improvements in farming efficiency and sustainability may increase as prices drop and adoption widens. Google's investment in quantum sensing highlights how innovative technology can support sustainable food production, helping farmers improve productivity and resilience in an unpredictable world.

Quantum computing for future technologies

Some of the most ambitious applications of quantum computing lie in fields that are still taking shape. Whether it's enabling deeper space missions, connecting the brain directly to machines, or building robots that respond intelligently to their surroundings, quantum systems could support breakthroughs that once felt out of reach.

Space exploration

A journey to Mars could take months less than it does today, guided by quantum-optimized trajectories that conserve fuel and maximize safety. Quantum computing might help us chart a future where the cosmos feels closer than ever.

Space exploration has always been driven by ambition and technological breakthroughs, with governments, private companies, and research institutions pushing the boundaries of human knowledge. As these efforts move closer to building lunar bases and, eventually, missions to Mars, the space industry's value is projected to exceed $1 trillion by 2040; a figure driven by technological advances and growing private investment.

The journey into space began with intense competition, known as the space race, primarily between the United States and the Soviet Union. In the early days, sending the first living creatures into space (including Laika, the Soviet dog) paved the way for human exploration. This race reached its peak with the historic 1969 moon landing, a moment that symbolized human ingenuity and the drive to push beyond Earth's boundaries. Since then, international cooperation has become central to space exploration, as seen in the International Space Station (ISS). This orbiting laboratory, managed jointly by space agencies from the United States, Russia, Europe, Japan, and Canada, serves as a research hub, allowing astronauts and scientists to conduct experiments on topics ranging from physics to biology in microgravity.

Meanwhile, advanced telescopes like the Hubble Space Telescope and the recently launched James Webb Space Telescope (JWST) reveal additional details about distant galaxies, star formation, and planetary systems. With each discovery, these telescopes generate new questions, increasing the need for sophisticated tools like quantum computing to solve previously unmanageable challenges. As humanity looks further into space, toward Mars and beyond, quantum computing offers promising ways to overcome these hurdles.

Quantum computing has become a powerful tool to handle many of the challenges in space exploration. Since the Apollo era, classical computing has been essential in space missions. However, as our ambitions stretch further, the limitations of traditional computing become more apparent. Quantum computing, with its advanced calculations, can address challenges from mission planning and trajectory optimization to data analysis, making space science more efficient.

Trajectory planning is a core challenge in space exploration, requiring precise calculations to guide spacecraft through complex paths, such as gravity assists or long-distance journeys. Quantum computing's ability to process many variables at once can significantly enhance trajectory optimization, helping craft faster and more fuel-efficient routes. QuAIL (NASA's Quantum AI Lab) is exploring quantum algorithms for orbital calculations and real-time adjustments. This capability is essential for deep-space missions, where mid-course corrections help spacecraft navigate gravitational fields efficiently and avoid hazards. By optimizing trajectories, quantum computing not only saves time and fuel but also improves mission safety and accuracy.

Fuel efficiency and resource management are also key areas where quantum computing can make a difference. Space agencies and companies, including NASA, **SpaceX**, and Airbus, are investigating ways to minimize fuel consumption while maximizing performance. Quantum computing's advanced simulations enable spacecraft to conserve energy by plotting optimal routes, and adjusting in real-time as conditions change. This improved resource efficiency supports long-term goals, such as deep-space missions and potential Mars colonies, by reducing the need for fuel resupply and allowing spacecraft to operate longer.

Quantum computing is also changing how we model extraterrestrial environments. Traditional simulations often struggle with the great number of factors involved in planetary systems, atmospheric conditions, and geological features. With quantum technology, multiple factors can be processed simultaneously, leading to more accurate simulations. For example, NASA and Google are researching quantum simulations to model the atmosphere on Mars and Jupiter's moon, Europa. This enhanced understanding helps scientists select landing sites, identify resources, and evaluate potential hazards, all of which are critical for planning future missions.

In the search for habitable worlds, quantum computing accelerates the analysis of the enormous data collected by telescopes like JWST. Astronomers are focused on finding planets within the **Goldilocks Zone**; the area around a star where temperatures are "just right" for liquid water to exist. Planets in this habitable zone are prime candidates for life, making them a top priority. Quantum computing can analyze factors such as orbital distance, atmosphere, and surface temperature faster than traditional methods, helping identify Earth-like planets. When combined with advanced AI, astronomers can sort through exoplanetary data more efficiently, moving closer to the goal of finding potentially habitable planets.

This idea of the "just right" zone even has a counterpart in science fiction. In Star Trek, Mr. Spock coined the term **M-class planet** for worlds with conditions similar to Earth, such as breathable air, moderate climates, and liquid water. This concept has inspired public interest in real-world astrobiology, guiding the search for Earth-like planets in our galaxy.

Quantum communication offers unique advantages for space exploration, particularly in secure, long-distance transmissions. The quantum property of quantum entanglement may allow for instant, secure communication, essential for far-reaching missions. China's quantum satellite Micius has already shown secure quantum communication over long distances, and agencies like NASA and the **European Space Agency (ESA)** are investigating similar techniques for interplanetary communication.

Besides these applications, quantum computing contributes to material science by supporting the development of spacecraft materials that are both durable and lightweight. Airbus is using quantum simulations to identify materials capable of withstanding extreme conditions in space. By testing atomic structures, quantum technology can help produce resilient materials that extend spacecraft lifespans and reduce the need for costly repairs or replacements.

The potential for autonomous space missions is another exciting development. As missions extend further from Earth, spacecraft will need to make independent decisions in real-time, adjusting to changing conditions without waiting for input from mission control. Quantum computers, working alongside AI, could support this autonomy, allowing, for example, a Mars rover to adapt to unexpected terrain and weather without needing immediate instructions from Earth. This ability will be essential for missions to distant planets, where communication delays can hinder effective decision-making.

Quantum computing offers alternative approaches to some of the most intricate problems in space science. From refining trajectories and improving resource management to ensuring secure communication and designing durable materials, quantum technology can enhance efficiency, security, and autonomy in space missions. By combining quantum advancements with AI and advanced networks, humanity can take the next steps in exploring deeper into the cosmos.

Brain-machine interfaces (BMIs)

Visualize communicating through thought alone, or controlling prosthetics as naturally as your own limbs. Quantum computing could take brain-machine interfaces to the next level, making them more intuitive, precise, and accessible to everyone.

Brain-machine interfaces (BMIs) connect human brain activity directly to external devices, allowing people to control computers, operate prosthetics, and communicate through thought alone. Initially an experimental field, BMIs have progressed significantly because of advancements in AI, machine learning, and neurotechnology. These tools have deepened our understanding of the brain and have helped make BMIs practical for various applications. Quantum computing also shows potential to enhance BMIs, particularly in managing issues like signal processing, noise reduction, and real-time adaptation.

The BMI field extends across healthcare, rehabilitation, entertainment, and defense, with a strong impact on individuals with disabilities. For the healthcare sector, BMIs assist with mobility, communication, and improving quality of life. For those recovering from conditions like strokes or brain injuries, quantum-enhanced BMIs could one day support neurorehabilitation. By providing therapists with a clearer, real-time view of brain recovery, they could enable treatments that adapt as the brain heals. Beyond healthcare, BMIs open possibilities for human-computer interaction in virtual and augmented reality (VR/AR), creating opportunities for training, entertainment, and education. The global BMI market, expected to reach $3.5 billion by 2027, is drawing substantial investments from companies, research institutions, and governments.

Many organizations are pushing BMI technology forward. **Neuralink**, founded by Elon Musk, focuses on developing implantable BMIs that aim to restore motor function and enable direct device communication, initially helping people with spinal cord injuries. Blackrock Neurotech specializes in neuroprosthetics, creating technology that enables paralyzed individuals to regain movement control through brain signals. Another company, Synchron, has developed a neural interface, the Stentrode, which can be implanted via blood vessels, reducing risks associated with open-brain surgery and making BMI technology more accessible. Meanwhile, Meta's Reality Labs (formerly Facebook Reality Labs) explores non-invasive BMIs to let users interact with VR/AR devices through thought. Their consumer-friendly, wearable technology could make BMIs a common feature in everyday digital interactions. Universities like MIT, Stanford, and UC Berkeley are also driving BMI advancements, particularly in neuroengineering and exploring quantum computing's potential to improve signal processing and neuroimaging accuracy, enabling BMIs to expand into new applications.

Quantum computing could address several critical issues in BMI technology, particularly in areas like signal processing, real-time adaptation, and neuroimaging. One of the major challenges BMIs face is accurately interpreting brain signals, which are often weak and affected by "noise" from other neural activity or external interference. Quantum computing could help filter and clarify these signals by processing large datasets in parallel, making BMIs more precise and responsive. For instance, IBM is researching **quantum noise** reduction for biomedical signals, which could make BMI-controlled devices easier to manage, benefiting those who use prosthetics, communication aids, or AR/VR interfaces.

Quantum computing could also enhance real-time adaptation in BMIs. Current BMIs rely on AI to translate brain signals into commands, but keeping up with the brain's rapid fluctuations is challenging. Quantum machine learning could enable real-time recalibration, making BMI interactions feel more natural and intuitive. This ability would be especially helpful for people who need to perform detailed tasks, such as typing, operating machinery, or even piloting drones. For individuals with neurological conditions where brain activity changes unpredictably, real-time adaptation could significantly improve the usability of BMIs.

Another promising application of quantum computing lies in neuroimaging, which is essential for achieving the fine-tuned control needed in BMIs. Traditional neuroimaging techniques like fMRI and EEG provide useful information but lack the precision required for more advanced BMI functions. Quantum-enhanced imaging could map neural pathways with greater accuracy, refining control over BMI devices and enabling more targeted interventions. Leading institutions, including MIT and Stanford, are investigating how quantum models might improve neuroimaging, potentially linking brain areas with specific actions and emotional responses. This expanded understanding of the brain could support BMIs designed to help users perform complex tasks, benefiting individuals with severe mobility limitations.

BMIs powered by quantum computing are expected to be beneficial for real-world applications that could significantly impact users. For people with paralysis, BMI implants from organizations such as Blackrock Neurotech enable control over robotic limbs, powered wheelchairs, and computers. With quantum-enhanced signal processing, these devices could become even more responsive, enabling smoother, more natural movement with less cognitive strain. In the AR/VR field, Meta's research into BMIs envisions environments where users can interact with virtual objects through thought alone. Quantum processing could make this interaction smoother and faster, enabling highly immersive experiences. Quantum neuroimaging could even allow BMIs to monitor mood and emotional states, offering applications in mental health. By identifying neural patterns associated with mood shifts, BMIs might one day provide real-time therapeutic feedback, supporting emotional well-being.

Looking further ahead, quantum computing in BMIs could lead to personalized devices that adapt to individual brain dynamics. Envision a BMI that assists an ALS patient in communicating through subtle neural signals, adjusting as their brain activity shifts with the disease's progression. Or a device that monitors stress and fatigue in real-time, offering support to manage mental well-being. Quantum-enhanced neuroimaging could allow BMIs to tune their responses to each person's unique neural patterns, making interactions with devices feel natural and efficient.

However, with BMI advancements come ethical and privacy considerations, particularly as quantum computing enables deeper insights into the brain. Privacy safeguards will be essential, as quantum-powered BMIs could access sensitive neural data. Quantum-safe encryption, now in development, could secure this data, preventing unauthorized access and protecting user privacy.

The fusion of quantum computing and BMI technology is opening a new era in human-technology interaction. By improving signal processing, enabling real-time adaptation, and advancing brain mapping, quantum computing could expand BMI applications beyond medical uses. It could support new methods of communication, entertainment, and mental health, making it possible to interact with the world through thought alone. With ongoing progress, BMIs could become as seamless and natural as any other form of human interaction, reshaping how we connect with technology and each other.

Robotics and automation

The future could see swarms of autonomous robots working together like a hive of bees; resilient, coordinated, and adaptive. Quantum computing may provide the brainpower needed to make robots truly responsive and effective in dynamic environments.

The robotics and automation industry forms the backbone of today's manufacturing, healthcare, transportation, and personal assistance sectors. With AI's rapid development, robots now perform a range of sophisticated tasks and make decisions in real-time. Yet, many robotic systems remain limited by current computing speeds and processing power, especially in fast-paced, unpredictable environments. Here, quantum computing enters as a game-changer, promising to enhance decision-making, streamline processes, and allow real-time adjustments that traditional systems can't handle.

Recent advancements have brought humanoid robots closer to reality. For example, Boston Dynamics' Atlas robot shows impressive agility and balance, performing tasks like running and jumping with human-like coordination. Similarly, Tesla's Optimus robot is designed to handle repetitive or hazardous tasks, with the potential to make a significant impact. These developments highlight the industry's progress toward creating robots capable of seamlessly integrating into human environments.

An exciting area is swarm robotics, which draws inspiration from nature; like ants, bees, and fish that work together in large groups to achieve complex goals without a single leader. In swarm robotics, multiple smaller robots collaborate autonomously, forming a flexible network capable of tackling tasks that a single robot might struggle with. For instance, in disaster relief, a swarm of drones could work together to scan an area, locate survivors, and deliver supplies to hard-to-reach places. Quantum computing could play a key role here by helping these swarms coordinate more efficiently, quickly calculating the optimal path, formation, or task allocation as conditions change. This approach could lead to more responsive, adaptable robotic systems in a variety of applications.

As a leader in robotic engineering, Boston Dynamics focuses on improving robots' stability and precision on uneven or shifting ground using advanced mechanical design and classical algorithms. Quantum-enhanced algorithms, while still in early development for robotics, hold the potential to further enhance these capabilities in the future.

Waymo, known for its advancements in autonomous driving, focuses on refining how its vehicles navigate changing road conditions through AI-driven route planning. These systems enable quicker, safer decision-making under various traffic and environmental scenarios. In the future, quantum computing could further enhance route optimization, potentially allowing autonomous vehicles to respond even more dynamically to complex road environments. NVIDIA, a top AI hardware provider, is researching quantum machine learning (QML) for advanced data processing, allowing robots to interact more fluidly with their environments. In manufacturing, ABB and Siemens are using quantum algorithms to optimize robotic workflows, enabling factories to adapt production on the fly, cutting down on waste and boosting efficiency.

One major obstacle for robots across sectors is the need to make split-second decisions. For instance, autonomous healthcare robots assisting patients or autonomous vehicles in heavy traffic must respond immediately. Traditional computing systems can struggle with these demands, often lagging in high-speed, dynamic scenarios. Robots navigating crowded warehouses or busy streets must plan the best route and avoid obstacles, all in real time. Quantum computing, however, can calculate and compare multiple paths at once, allowing robots to adjust their course instantly when new information (like a moving pedestrian or a new obstacle) comes into view. Suppose we have a robotic assistant in a hospital corridor, wheeling medication to a patient's room. If a nurse steps in front of it or a gurney blocks its path, the robot recalculates and chooses an alternate route in milliseconds; reacting smoothly and naturally, much like a human would. Quantum computing makes this kind of responsiveness more achievable.

In cluttered or low-visibility spaces, robots also need to distinguish objects quickly and accurately, whether it's a logistics robot sorting packages or a medical robot identifying tissues during surgery. Quantum-enhanced AI could dramatically improve object recognition by processing visual data with higher precision and speed. This ability would allow a logistics robot to work in dark, crowded environments or a surgical robot to pinpoint vital areas without hesitation.

Quantum technology also offers promising applications in predictive maintenance. Factories, for example, depend on automated systems that require constant monitoring to prevent breakdowns. While traditional AI can analyze patterns to predict when a machine part might fail, quantum computing's parallel processing can evaluate many factors simultaneously leading to faster, more precise predictions. In a busy production facility, this means a quantum-AI system could flag a robotic arm needing attention before it causes a costly delay, optimizing maintenance schedules and minimizing downtime.

IBM is collaborating with major companies to develop quantum algorithms that automate supply chains. In automated warehouses, quantum-powered AI can help manage inventory, sort products, and adjust restocking needs in real-time. Envision a system that packs and ships goods as soon as they're ordered, handling thousands of items with unmatched speed and accuracy. This approach is pushing warehouse efficiency to unthinkable levels, allowing for faster delivery and better service.

The future of robotics may even see fully adaptive machines, robots capable of learning and responding instantly to shifting conditions. For example, think of a production-line robot that changes its movements depending on the specific demands of each item it handles. These adaptive robots could become valuable in fields that require versatile, real-time adjustments, as quantum systems empower them to interpret new data and shift accordingly.

As the robotics and automation industry moves forward, quantum computing may introduce unprecedented levels of precision, flexibility, and speed. In many ways, it's like *boldly going where no robot has gone before*, into a future where machines work alongside humans in ways that feel almost natural. Quantum-driven robotics may soon advance industries, allowing robots to operate with precision and adaptability that push the boundaries of what's possible.

The societal impact of quantum computing

As quantum computing advances, important questions arise about its wider effects on society. Like other major technologies, quantum computing offers exciting potential but also raises concerns, such as ethical issues, security risks, and impacts on education and the environment.

Ethical and security implications

Quantum computing's ability to break current encryption methods presents serious concerns about data privacy, security, and national defense. Today's digital systems rely on encryption algorithms that, for classical computers, would take an unrealistic amount of time to crack. Quantum computers, however, with their power to perform large-scale calculations swiftly, could threaten these defenses. This would leave sensitive information, from personal data and financial records to state secrets, exposed to potential misuse, creating significant risks for individuals, businesses, and governments.

To counter this, researchers are developing quantum-safe encryption algorithms designed to withstand quantum attacks. Known as post-quantum cryptography, these algorithms aim to secure data in a future world with quantum technology. Transitioning critical systems worldwide to quantum-safe encryption is no small task, requiring substantial collaboration across markets, governments, and sectors. If you consider replacing every lock in the world with a newer, stronger model, this reflects the scale and effort needed. Beyond the technical hurdles, this shift will demand considerable funding and political support to make post-quantum cryptography a widespread reality.

As quantum capabilities advance, concerns about privacy increase. In a world where quantum algorithms could rapidly decode encrypted information, individuals and organizations would face additional difficulties in safeguarding sensitive data. Quantum-enhanced analysis could reveal personal details or corporate secrets, making privacy breaches more challenging to manage and potentially eroding trust in digital systems.

Quantum technology also complicates data sovereignty, the principle that a citizen's data should remain within their home country. With global quantum networks, maintaining this standard becomes more difficult, as quantum systems may process data beyond national borders. International agreements may be necessary to address these issues, setting guidelines for data storage, processing, and access in a quantum-powered world. Similar to the **European Union's AI Act**, which sets ethical standards for AI, future policies for quantum technology could require transparency, accountability, and ethical standards to ensure that this technology serves the public interest. Organizations might need to assess the risks of data exposure and put protocols in place to prevent misuse, adding protective measures around quantum decryption and data security.

The EU's AI Act offers principles that could guide the regulation of quantum technology, emphasizing transparency, fair access, and risk management. For transparency, clear guidelines could ensure that quantum processes are understandable, particularly in areas like finance, healthcare, and national security, where clarity is crucial for public trust and oversight.

For fair access, regulations could prevent monopolies by supporting open-source platforms and enabling widespread involvement in quantum research, similar to the AI Act's aim to ensure equitable access to technology. This approach would encourage collaboration, broadening the benefits of quantum advancements.

Risk management is particularly relevant, given the unique data security challenges posed by quantum technology. A regulatory framework could require developers to proactively address these risks, especially in areas concerning public safety and data protection, ensuring that potential vulnerabilities are minimized.

Together, these actions could create a balanced environment for quantum development, promoting innovation while safeguarding the public interest.

Quantum computing demands significant resources, infrastructure, and expertise, raising concerns that only well-funded entities may dominate this technology, potentially creating inequities. If access to quantum remains limited to the most well-resourced organizations, the digital divide could widen, allowing larger corporations or countries to control critical sectors.

Exclusive access to quantum tools could give certain players a competitive edge in fields like financial forecasting, materials science, and AI; opportunities that smaller nations or organizations might find out of reach. This imbalance could deepen global power divides, with quantum-enabled countries gaining advantages that others struggle to bridge.

Addressing these issues will call for global cooperation. Just as international treaties regulate nuclear and space technologies, agreements on quantum computing could help ensure the technology's benefits are shared more widely. Collaborative research hubs, modeled after centers like CERN, could offer open-access environments, enabling a broader range of countries and institutions to benefit from quantum advancements and reducing monopolistic risks.

The ethical challenges of quantum computing call to mind the **Prime Directive** in Star Trek, where advanced civilizations are bound by rules that prevent interference with less developed societies. Just as the **Federation** avoids imposing its technology and culture on others, a similar principle might guide the responsible use of quantum technology. Nations could agree to practice restraint, ensuring that quantum advancements don't disrupt global balances or widen inequalities. A "quantum directive" could serve as a reminder to prioritize global stability and respect for sovereignty, encouraging technology-sharing practices that align with the greater good rather than individual advantage.

Creating frameworks for responsible quantum use could help build global trust and stability. Organizations like the United Nations or the World Economic Forum could lead these initiatives, bringing countries together to establish ethical and security standards. Similar to treaties on nuclear or space technology, such agreements could offer guidelines to prevent misuse, encourage transparency, and promote peaceful applications of quantum technology, easing competitive tensions.

These efforts involve balancing national interests, economic goals, and ethical considerations. However, a united approach could provide substantial benefits, from building public trust in quantum technology to creating an environment where all countries can share in its potential.

Open-source quantum platforms could make a notable difference in making quantum resources more accessible. Platforms like IBM's **Qiskit** and Rigetti's Forest provide free quantum computing tools, allowing researchers, students, and developers to work with quantum technology without needing costly resources. Expanding these platforms through global partnerships could allow more countries and organizations to benefit, reducing the risk of monopolistic control.

Governments could also consider intergovernmental agreements on software and hardware standards for quantum computing. Much like the internet, which was built on shared protocols like TCP/IP, quantum computing could benefit from standardized approaches to support global interoperability and security. Open standards would allow quantum systems to work together, providing fair access to these technologies.

Quantum computing has the potential to revolutionize industries, enhance security, and solve scientific challenges. To realize this potential while protecting public interests, a cooperative approach is essential. By supporting open-access platforms, ethical guidelines, and promoting global collaboration, we can prevent imbalances of power and ensure that quantum technology serves society.

With shared resources, collective knowledge, and cooperative policies, the international community can aim for a future where quantum computing promotes unity, encouraging a fair and secure world.

Education and workforce development

Quantum computing is reshaping the skills schools and universities need to prepare students for future demands. Unlike traditional computing, quantum introduces unique ideas like superposition and quantum entanglement, which require a fresh way of thinking. Just as computer literacy became essential, "quantum literacy" is also becoming necessary, urging educational institutions to adapt.

In the world of Star Trek, **Starfleet Academy** serves as the training ground for future officers of the United Federation of Planets. Students are taught to handle advanced technology, uphold ethical standards, and work across diverse fields, from engineering and medicine to diplomacy. Much like preparing cadets at Starfleet, building a quantum-ready workforce means developing a blend of technical skill and social awareness that can adapt to the unknown. Schools today face a similar task in training students not only in quantum fundamentals but also in understanding the wider impact of this technology.

Preparing for a quantum-powered world involves a range of skills beyond just training quantum physicists. Much like AI and software development, which rely on coding, data science, ethics, and policy expertise, quantum computing will need software engineers, data scientists, cybersecurity specialists, and policymakers with a basic understanding of quantum principles.

Universities have started offering courses in quantum computing, and, for example, IBM and Google have launched accessible quantum learning programs. Expanding these programs to high schools and even middle schools will be crucial. Teaching quantum concepts such as superposition and quantum entanglement alongside physics and computer science will give young students a head start, equipping them to understand a world increasingly influenced by quantum technology.

Just as AI led to specialized training in machine learning and data science, quantum computing will likely inspire targeted programs in areas like quantum software development, hardware engineering, and the ethics of quantum technology. Schools and universities could create programs that combine technical skills with lessons on the societal impact of quantum, preparing students for various roles.

This approach would not only produce technical experts but also professionals "quantum-aware" across fields such as law, business, and policy. For instance, law students might learn quantum basics to handle legal matters related to intellectual property and regulations, while business students could explore the effects of quantum on markets. This broader training can help build a workforce ready to support quantum technology across different sectors.

Quantum computing faces similar issues to those encountered with technologies like AI. Just as AI raised concerns about data privacy, job shifts, and surveillance, quantum may also disrupt jobs and skill needs, creating new opportunities but possibly leaving some people behind. By learning from AI's challenges, quantum developers and policymakers can take early steps to manage risks and support fair development.

Because of the extensive resources required for quantum research, international partnerships will be vital to building a skilled workforce. Much like the global cooperation seen in AI or climate initiatives, collaboration in quantum could expand access to education and job opportunities. Some countries have already launched national quantum programs, but a shared approach could provide broader access to quantum training. Nations with established programs could offer scholarships, internships, and exchange opportunities to students and professionals from other regions, creating a globally skilled workforce.

As quantum technology progresses, ethical considerations will grow increasingly important. Preparing people for this field means focusing on both technical knowledge and ethics. Quantum professionals will need to understand the societal impacts of their work, from data privacy to fair access. Schools and organizations could establish ethical guidelines for quantum, similar to those in AI, to encourage responsible practices.

Embedding ethics into quantum education can produce a workforce that's not only skilled but also sensitive to broader concerns. Those trained with both quantum and ethical perspectives will be better prepared to manage the challenges posed by this powerful technology, ensuring it develops in a way that serves the public interest.

Environmental considerations

Quantum computers need extremely low temperatures (close to absolute zero) to keep qubits stable and functioning accurately. This level of cooling is energy-intensive, raising concerns about sustainability as quantum computing grows. Addressing these energy demands without creating new environmental issues is essential as we work to unlock the potential of this technology.

Cooling quantum computers is one of the most challenging environmental hurdles. Superconducting qubits, for example, need to be near absolute zero, requiring specialized cryogenic systems that consume significant energy. Some companies, like Microsoft, are researching alternative qubit designs, such as topological qubits, which may require less cooling or operate at higher temperatures. Meanwhile, Honeywell's trapped-ion technology operates at slightly warmer conditions, which could also reduce cooling demands. If these room-temperature and near-room-temperature qubit technologies advance, the environmental impact of quantum computing could decrease substantially.

Researchers are increasingly looking to nature for sustainable solutions. Photosynthesis, for instance, shows an example of efficient energy use in nature. Some plants and bacteria convert sunlight into energy with minimal waste by using a quantum effect that resembles coherence. In this process, particles generated by sunlight transfer energy along highly efficient pathways, enabling energy to reach the cell's reaction center with minimal loss. Inspired by this, scientists are exploring ways to design quantum systems that use energy just as efficiently.

If Star Trek taught us anything, it's that advanced technology and environmental responsibility go hand-in-hand. Much like how the USS Enterprise powers its warp core using matter-antimatter reactions to generate immense energy with minimal waste, quantum computing is exploring ways to achieve powerful results while keeping its environmental impact low. Just as the Federation has strict protocols to avoid unnecessary harm, quantum researchers are designing systems that channel energy efficiently, reducing waste and aiming for sustainability.

IBM and Google are already investigating ways to limit quantum computing's environmental footprint. IBM, for instance, is working on making their dilution refrigerators (essential for keeping quantum processors cool) more energy-efficient. Google is exploring ways to integrate renewable energy into their quantum labs, aligning with their broader sustainability goals. These initiatives aim to create scalable quantum computing infrastructures without an overwhelming carbon footprint.

In the push for sustainability, quantum computing facilities are also looking to data centers as a model for renewable energy use. Data centers increasingly use wind, solar, and hydropower to cut their carbon footprints, and some quantum labs are following suit. IBM has committed to powering its global operations, including quantum facilities, entirely with renewable energy by 2030. Google is also pursuing 24/7 carbon-free energy for its data centers, a goal that could extend to quantum computing as well. Researchers are even exploring ways to capture and recycle waste heat from quantum cooling systems, similar to how some data centers use excess heat to power secondary systems, creating a circular energy model.

Beyond cooling and energy use, scientists are also looking closely at the materials used in quantum technology. Many current components rely on rare earth elements and metals that must be mined or chemically refined. These processes can cause habitat destruction, toxic runoff, and high carbon emissions. The sourcing of such materials often involves environmental and ethical concerns. In response, some research is focused on biomaterials, which are made from biological sources, to reduce dependence on traditional extraction and processing. Bio-based polymers, for example, may one day replace conventional materials in quantum components while offering durability and potential biodegradability. Researchers are also exploring "green chemistry" techniques that aim to produce quantum-grade materials with less waste and fewer harmful byproducts. This work could help set new standards for environmentally responsible manufacturing in quantum hardware.

Another consideration is the lifecycle of quantum hardware. Quantum systems contain rare materials like niobium and tantalum, which are difficult to recycle and potentially harmful if not disposed of properly. To mitigate this, researchers are exploring more sustainable material alternatives and developing recycling programs to reclaim rare elements from outdated quantum systems. This approach mirrors the electronics industry's shift toward recycling rare minerals from old devices, where, for instance, Apple now reclaims rare metals from returned iPhones.

While these efforts are still developing, they show that the quantum computing industry is aware of its environmental responsibilities. Drawing inspiration from the Federation's values in Star Trek, which emphasize progress alongside ethical responsibility, the industry can work toward creating quantum technology that aligns with these principles. By doing so, we could make strides toward a more sustainable future, where quantum computing benefits humanity without compromising the planet.

Global collaboration and quantum diplomacy

Quantum computing today resembles a high-stakes race, with countries pursuing different strategies to secure leadership in this rapidly advancing field. Just as space exploration once shifted global dynamics, the "quantum race" is sparking new alliances and challenges. The United States and Europe focus on developing powerful quantum computers, while China has made impressive strides in quantum communication and encryption. Each region's emphasis highlights its unique priorities and strategy for advancing this technology.

In the United States, the National Quantum Initiative Act has driven significant funding into quantum research. Major tech companies, including IBM, Google, and Microsoft, collaborate with universities and national labs to advance quantum hardware and software. IBM has developed increasingly capable quantum processors, while Google reached a milestone called "quantum supremacy", where their processor solved a problem that classical computers would find almost impossible to complete. These achievements underline the U.S. commitment to maintaining leadership in computing power.

Europe, through the **Quantum Flagship** program, has invested €1 billion over ten years in supporting quantum research, encouraging partnerships, and cultivating a skilled workforce. This initiative strengthens Europe's position in quantum innovation by enabling collaborations across countries and disciplines. Canada, too, is an active player, with the University of Waterloo's Institute for Quantum Computing and organizations such as D-Wave focusing on practical applications of quantum technology.

China has taken a unique approach, prioritizing quantum communication and encryption. State-backed projects have enabled China to achieve milestones such as launching the first quantum satellite, Micius, which facilitates secure, long-distance quantum communication; a groundbreaking step in secure global data transmission. Just as advanced communication systems protect sensitive information in a complex, interconnected world, China's focus on encryption could redefine secure global communications.

A unified "quantum-safe" communication system is becoming increasingly important. Without common standards, countries may develop encryption methods that don't align, complicating secure communication. An international agreement on quantum encryption standards would prevent fragmented approaches and enable safe data-sharing across borders, much like how shared technologies and ethical values in collaborative organizations support cooperative, peaceful communication.

Some experts suggest that international quantum research centers, modeled after CERN in particle physics, could offer neutral ground for global collaboration. Such centers could receive global funding, providing equal access to advanced quantum resources and supporting open-source platforms. Expanding tools like IBM's Qiskit and Rigetti's Forest software would make quantum technology more accessible and help avoid monopolization of this field.

Building a strong workforce for quantum technology also depends on collaboration. As demand grows for quantum scientists, engineers, and developers, international exchange programs, online courses, and research fellowships will help expand the pool of skilled professionals. Some countries are already integrating quantum concepts into high school curriculums. For instance, the EU's Quantum Flagship aims to introduce basic quantum principles to high school students, offering young learners an early start in this field.

While each nation has specific goals, global cooperation and shared ethical standards will be essential to avoid a quantum arms race and ensure this technology benefits society. Just as responsible sharing of knowledge is crucial in avoiding harm, international efforts can balance national interests with humanity's broader needs. This approach could turn quantum computing into a bridge for global cooperation, addressing challenges in health, climate, and security.

By guiding quantum technology with a shared vision and ethical standards, humanity can shape a future where this powerful tool serves everyone.

Quantum computing roadmap

As quantum computing advances, the possibilities seem nearly limitless. From new qubit designs and refined error correction techniques to hybrid systems combining classical and quantum processors, each step forward brings us closer to practical applications that could reform entire fields. This chapter explores where quantum computing may be headed, focusing on technical advancements on the horizon, the potential of **hybrid quantum-classical systems**, and a realistic look at where the technology might stand in the next two decades.

Progress toward quantum computing's full potential

Quantum computing is advancing through focused research that aims to make these systems more powerful, stable, and scalable. A major area of effort is improving qubit design, with researchers testing different types to increase reliability. Superconducting qubits and trapped ions are currently leading the field, but topological qubits are also gaining attention.

Topological qubits use a special approach based on the mathematics of topology, which studies properties that remain unchanged even when objects are stretched or reshaped. In this context, information is stored in the global properties of a system rather than in a specific physical state. This makes topological qubits naturally resistant to many types of errors that affect other qubit designs. The idea is that by protecting information in this way, quantum operations become more stable and less likely to break down during a calculation.

Topological qubits are still in the experimental stage, but if successful, they could support more complex computations with fewer qubits and less need for correction. Companies such as Microsoft are actively exploring this approach as a path toward scalable and fault-tolerant quantum computing.

Another essential area of development is error correction. Quantum systems are particularly sensitive to environmental influences, making it difficult to maintain coherence; the balanced state in which qubits work in harmony. Unlike classical computers, which can apply straightforward error correction techniques, quantum systems require additional qubits dedicated to real-time error detection and correction. This constant correction is necessary for quantum computers to manage the intricate calculations they're designed to solve.

A practical approach gaining attention in the field is the hybrid quantum-classical system, which combines the strengths of quantum and classical computing to maximize their unique benefits. This setup is one of the most promising near-term applications, allowing quantum and classical components to collaborate, each handling tasks that best suit its abilities. Classical computers manage the overarching process, including tasks like data preparation, preliminary calculations, and communication between quantum and classical parts, while quantum processors manage specific tasks that rely on quantum properties like parallelism.

In a typical hybrid system, the classical computer is the orchestrator. It organizes, cleans, and structures data into formats compatible with quantum computing. For instance, classical processors handle pre- and post-processing tasks, such as data encoding, splitting the workload, and ensuring each system focuses on its strengths. For problems requiring optimization, the classical computer might generate an initial solution and pass it to the quantum processor for refinement. The quantum processor then uses superposition and quantum entanglement to explore multiple solutions simultaneously; a feat classical processors struggle to achieve.

After the quantum computation, results are sent back to the classical system, which translates these quantum outputs into interpretable data. Since quantum results are often probabilistic or encoded in quantum states, this step is crucial to making the results usable. Classical systems also play a significant role in error management, detecting and correcting inconsistencies to improve stability. This collaboration often creates an iterative feedback loop: the classical computer refines instructions based on intermediate results, adjusting and re-sending tasks to the quantum processor until reaching an optimal solution. In this way, hybrid systems provide a realistic pathway to leveraging quantum technology's computational strengths without placing all demands on quantum systems alone.

Progress in quantum algorithms is equally crucial. Algorithms like Shor's (for factoring) and Grover's (for search) were instrumental in demonstrating the unique potential of quantum computing. Building on these foundations, researchers are now developing algorithms to tackle broader real-world applications, such as cryptography and data analysis. This ongoing expansion in quantum algorithms is fundamental to unlocking quantum computing's potential for various industries. For readers interested in a deeper dive, these algorithms and their uses are discussed further in Appendix A: Essential tools and techniques in quantum programming.

Quantum hardware innovations are also driving the field forward. Researchers are improving not only qubits but also the physical environments that house them. Advanced cryogenic systems and vacuum chambers, for example, provide stable, isolated environments for qubits, reducing the risk of errors from external interference. These improvements in quantum hardware are essential for supporting the delicate quantum states qubits rely on to function accurately.

In quantum networking and communication, efforts such as quantum key distribution (QKD), which we previously discussed in the context of cybersecurity, aim to create ultra-secure communication channels that could eventually link quantum systems into a **quantum internet**. Quantum networks could offer a level of security beyond classical systems, with applications ranging from national security to financial data protection.

Beyond QKD, other advancements in quantum communication focus on quantum entanglement, allowing data to be shared instantly across distances, a process called quantum teleportation. China's Micius satellite has already shown some of these possibilities, using entangled photons to enable secure communication across hundreds of miles. While still experimental, such techniques hint at future secure networks where data could be theoretically impossible to intercept or alter. These advancements could show the way for a global quantum internet, linking quantum computers and sensors across significant distances with unprecedented security and speed.

As mentioned in the earlier chapter on the intersection of AI and quantum computing, quantum machine learning (QML) merges quantum computing with AI to open new possibilities in data analysis, natural language processing, and pattern recognition. QML algorithms are expected to deliver processing speeds beyond those achievable by classical AI, potentially reshaping fields that rely on high-speed data analysis. For readers interested in a deeper exploration of QML, additional details are provided in Appendix B: Foundations of quantum machine learning.

Similarly, quantum simulation is gaining attention, as quantum computers are exceptionally well-suited to simulate molecular structures and reactions, tasks that are highly demanding for classical computers. Quantum simulation could lead to advancements in fields like drug discovery, materials science, and chemistry, enabling researchers to model molecular interactions with greater precision. These simulations may accelerate the development of new drugs and materials by uncovering molecular behaviors that were previously inaccessible.

As quantum systems grow, the field is also developing quantum programming languages and software tools. Platforms like Qiskit, Cirq, **Microsoft's Quantum Development Kit**, and Amazon Braket are designed to make quantum programming more accessible. These tools bridge the gap between advanced quantum hardware and real-world applications, supporting developers and researchers as they explore quantum computing's capabilities. Amazon Braket, in particular, operates on a quantum-as-a-service model, providing cloud-based access to a range of quantum devices, including those from IonQ and other providers. This service allows users to experiment with quantum algorithms and simulate quantum systems through an accessible platform, making it easier for organizations and developers to explore quantum technology without investing in specialized hardware.

Error mitigation techniques complement error correction by managing quantum errors in "noisy" systems, where full error correction might be impractical. Error mitigation strategies allow quantum systems to produce reliable results even with some inherent instability, making them particularly valuable for early quantum computers with limited qubit resources.

As we discussed in the chapter on precision agriculture, quantum sensors are becoming powerful tools for precise measurement in fields like healthcare, navigation, and environmental science. By leveraging quantum mechanics for high-sensitivity measurements, these sensors allow for greater accuracy in tracking physical properties like time, gravity, and magnetic fields, providing breakthroughs in areas where precision is critical.

Finally, topological quantum computing is pushing the boundaries of qubit design. Unlike conventional qubits, topological qubits encode information in a way that naturally resists environmental errors. Although still experimental, this approach holds potential for creating more robust, error-resistant qubits, which could significantly enhance the stability of future quantum computers.

Together, these advancements, from hybrid systems to topological qubits and error mitigation, reflect the wide-ranging efforts to develop practical, reliable quantum computing. As these innovations converge, they bring us closer to reaching "quantum advantage", where quantum computers surpass classical systems in solving specific, useful tasks. Quantum advantage builds on the idea of quantum supremacy, which, as discussed earlier, refers to the point at which a quantum computer can complete a calculation that would be infeasible for any classical system, even if the task itself isn't necessarily practical. Quantum supremacy is an important milestone, demonstrating the unique capabilities of quantum systems, and we are likely to see more instances of supremacy in specialized fields as quantum algorithms and hardware advance.

Achieving quantum advantage could be as groundbreaking as the Federation's first contact missions in Star Trek. These moments marked major expansions of knowledge, pushing the boundaries of what was known and possible. Similarly, quantum computing would open up new possibilities, enabling us to solve problems that seemed impossible with classical systems and leading to major changes in technology and science.

A timeline: milestones in quantum computing's future

Predicting the exact path of quantum computing is challenging. However, the rapid, exponential growth in technology, similar to the trend seen in classical computing, gives us an idea of what may unfold in the coming decades. As with past technological revolutions, this growth drives quantum computing's progress, allowing us to picture a future where its potential reaches nearly every field.

Current state: Experimental foundations (0-5 years)

Today's commercial quantum systems, generally containing around 50-100 qubits, are accessible through cloud platforms like Amazon Braket, IBM Quantum Platform, and Microsoft Azure Quantum. These systems are mainly used in research, allowing scientists to better understand quantum principles while addressing challenges such as error correction, coherence times, and qubit stability.

Quantum Machine Learning (QML) algorithms are in the early stages of testing, but they may lead to breakthroughs in various areas. In finance, researchers are exploring QML to improve predictive modeling, while in logistics, early algorithms are being tested to optimize supply chains. In healthcare, QML is being applied to classify complex datasets, with exciting potential in drug discovery. For example, quantum systems may soon allow researchers to predict atomic-level molecular interactions, accelerating the development of new treatments with unprecedented precision.

Next 5 years: Early commercialization and specialized applications (5-10 years)

Over the next five years, companies like IBM, Google, Microsoft, Rigetti, and IonQ are expected to advance qubit stability, error correction, and processor scaling. These improvements could support the first wave of commercial applications in multiple fields.

For the healthcare industry, quantum simulations of molecular structures could advance drug development by allowing researchers to predict molecular behavior with high accuracy. For the finance sector, QML algorithms may enhance risk assessment, enabling more precise market analysis and portfolio optimization. The logistics industry could experience significant changes as quantum-powered AI optimizes supply chain management, using real-time analysis to develop efficient schedules and route plans.

With the new data security concerns, blockchain and cryptography will require quantum-safe methods to secure blockchain integrity against quantum risks, and early quantum-resistant protocols may be tested during this period. Quantum applications in urban planning could help optimize traffic flow, energy use, and emergency response, promoting the growth of smart cities. In agriculture, quantum-enhanced AI may improve irrigation, soil monitoring, and crop yield predictions, contributing to sustainable farming.

10 years: Widespread adoption and integration (10-15 years)

In the decade ahead, quantum hardware may reach the stability needed for larger, reliable qubit systems with advanced error correction. Hybrid quantum-classical systems could become standard in fields that depend on complex simulations.

In climate science, quantum-enhanced AI models may improve long-term climate predictions, providing data-driven insights for environmental strategies. In materials science, quantum systems could enable simulations to discover new material properties, driving progress in custom manufacturing, electronics, and energy storage. Quantum-empowered cybersecurity systems may also advance encryption methods, securing data, which is essential in nearly every field.

Quantum computing could significantly aid space exploration. Quantum-AI systems may optimize mission logistics, resource management, and sustainable habitat design for long-term missions. In neurology, Brain-Machine Interfaces (BMIs) could use quantum processing to interpret neural signals with great accuracy, advancing neuroprosthetics and supporting new rehabilitation tools and thought-controlled devices.

15 years: Mature quantum-AI systems and new horizons (15-20 years)

In the long term, quantum computing and AI may integrate seamlessly, supporting applications that require complex decision-making, adaptive learning, and large-scale data analysis. Quantum-AI systems could drive advancements in autonomous robotics, environmental management, education, and neurology.

For example, quantum-powered robots may navigate complex environments autonomously, making real-time decisions in fields like manufacturing, transportation, and deep-space exploration. Neurology could benefit from quantum simulations of brain function, leading to new treatments for neurological disorders and expanded BMIs for cognitive enhancement. In precision agriculture, quantum-AI systems could monitor ecosystems in real-time, optimizing crop rotation, water management, and sustainable farming practices.

In education, QML could personalize learning environments by adapting to individual cognitive profiles, providing a tailored educational experience that aligns with each learner's needs.

20 years and beyond: Quantum-AI synergy shaping the future (20-30+ years)

As quantum computing advances toward its full potential, its impact may mirror the significant influence of classical computing in the late 20th century. It could shape industries, create new fields, and address some of humanity's most intricate challenges.

Quantum computing may drive breakthroughs in AI, producing faster, more adaptable systems capable of managing large-scale datasets. For the healthcare sector, quantum-enhanced AI might enable highly personalized treatments tailored at the molecular level. In finance, real-time economic modeling could help stabilize global markets. Brain-Machine Interfaces (BMIs) could make strides, supporting cognitive augmentation and brain-to-device communication, enabling individuals to interact with technology using thought alone.

Quantum cryptography and cybersecurity could also develop as quantum-safe cryptographic methods are widely adopted. These advancements could secure sensitive data across critical infrastructure, financial systems, and government communications, potentially leading to completely secure communication networks and a more stable global digital landscape.

For global sustainability, quantum computing offers unique tools for addressing resource management, renewable energy distribution, and climate change. Quantum-enhanced models could optimize energy grids, water distribution, and supply chains, making it possible to operate global systems more efficiently and sustainably.

In scientific exploration, quantum computing could deepen our understanding of fundamental laws by enabling simulations that reveal additional aspects of quantum mechanics and atomic interactions. This expanded understanding could drive advancements in materials science, physics, and cosmology.

As humanity looks toward space, Quantum-AI systems may be essential for long-term interplanetary missions and space colonization. Quantum simulations could support life-support designs, optimize resource use for sustainable habitats, and even aid in navigating and exploring new worlds.

This long-term perspective envisions quantum computing as a vital part of future infrastructure, enabling solutions to humanity's most challenging problems. Whether improving AI, strengthening cybersecurity, supporting sustainable development, or expanding scientific discovery, quantum computing's potential extends across nearly every field, helping shape a future that addresses complex and critical needs.

REFLECTIONS

Part III

Philosophical questions in quantum computing

Quantum computing is not just a technological breakthrough; it also pushes us to reconsider our understanding of reality, knowledge, and existence. Both philosophers and physicists have long been intrigued by the ideas behind quantum mechanics, which challenge fundamental assumptions about observation, existence, and causality. The strange and counterintuitive aspects of quantum mechanics raise discussions that go beyond science, making us reflect on what it means to know, to observe, and to understand our place in the universe. This chapter explores how quantum computing connects to these deeper ideas and its potential to reshape how we see the world.

One of the most famous aspects of quantum mechanics is the role of the observer in determining a particle's state. A particle such as an electron doesn't exist in one definite place or condition; instead, it exists as a probability wave, representing all possible states at once. This concept, known as superposition, highlights how observation collapses possibilities into a single reality, as previously discussed with Schrödinger's cat. The Apple TV+ series **Devs**, created by Alex Garland, explores this within a deterministic framework. Forest, played by Nick Offerman, believes that everything is predetermined and unfolds according to unchangeable laws. His perspective aligns with classical determinism but stands in contrast to the uncertainty found in quantum mechanics. When Forest declares, "Nothing ever changes. Everything happens the way it was always going to," he expresses his belief in a fully predictable universe. This raises an interesting thought: could quantum computing ever allow us to foresee reality with such certainty, or does the universe resist that level of predictability?

Quantum mechanics also introduces the idea of indeterminacy, some properties cannot be precisely known at the same time. Heisenberg's Uncertainty Principle states that knowing a particle's exact position means knowing less about its momentum, and vice versa. This brings up an important debate: is the universe completely predictable, or does quantum mechanics show that uncertainty is woven into reality itself? If randomness exists at the quantum level, does this suggest a form of unpredictability that challenges the classical idea that every event is strictly caused by what came before?

Quantum entanglement is another puzzling idea in quantum mechanics. When two particles are entangled, they become linked in a way that means the state of one instantly affects the state of the other, no matter how far apart they are. Albert Einstein called this "spooky action at a distance" because it doesn't follow the usual rules of cause and effect. In quantum computing, entanglement allows qubits to work together in ways classical bits can't, making quantum computers more powerful for certain problems. But entanglement also leads to questions: how can two particles stay connected over large distances? This challenges our understanding of how information and the universe work. It also makes us think about whether everything in the universe might be connected in ways we don't yet understand.

Quantum mechanics also introduces randomness into how particles behave. Some events are not strictly caused by what happened before. This goes against the classical view of a clockwork universe, where every event follows directly from the one before it. Instead, quantum mechanics suggests some things happen by chance, shaped by probabilities rather than certainties. You might ask whether this randomness shows that the universe is not as fixed as it seems and whether it leaves room for free will at the smallest levels of existence.

Quantum computing doesn't just raise scientific and philosophical concerns; it also has real-world consequences. For example, it could change cryptography and data security by breaking existing encryption methods, and forcing alternative approaches to cybersecurity. Beyond these practical issues, a broader ethical discussion arises: should there be limits to the knowledge we pursue, especially when it could lead to unintended consequences? Similar debates have occurred in fields like genetics and AI. With quantum computing, it may be up to researchers, governments, and international organizations to balance progress with responsibility.

Quantum mechanics and quantum computing challenge the way we think about reality. Does the quantum world reveal a deeper layer of existence, or is it simply a mathematical framework for solving certain problems? Superposition, entanglement, and uncertainty push the boundaries of our intuition, suggesting that reality at the smallest scales operates in ways we wouldn't expect. Stories like Devs and various philosophical perspectives remind us that quantum computing isn't just about building faster computers, it's also a window into deeper questions about existence, consciousness, and knowledge. As we continue to explore quantum science, we may find that it offers insights not only into advanced problem-solving but also into the nature of reality itself; ideas that have fascinated thinkers for centuries.

The philosophical implications of quantum computing remind us that this technology is more than just a tool, it's also a way to rethink what we know about reality. As we look ahead to the future of quantum computing and its impact on society, these deeper ideas will play a role in shaping how we approach its development and use.

Reflections on the future of quantum computing

Quantum computing represents a significant leap forward, changing how we think about technology and its role in addressing global challenges. Built on principles like superposition and entanglement, it expands the possibilities of computation into areas previously out of reach. As we've explored in this book, quantum technology has the potential to drive progress across industries, offering new tools to solve intricate problems. Now, let's reflect on where this progress might take us and its implications for the future.

By enabling faster and more precise calculations, quantum computing could change areas like medicine, sustainability, and innovation, helping us explore solutions to some of the most pressing questions facing society today.

As we've seen in this book, the combination of quantum computing and AI stands out as a powerful pairing. Quantum technology has the potential to expand AI's capacity for data analysis and prediction, making insights more precise. AI has already changed sectors by analyzing data, identifying patterns, and automating complex tasks. Now, quantum computing adds new capabilities, allowing AI to manage enormous datasets, model detailed real-world scenarios, and even support the development of future quantum algorithms and hardware. This collaboration has promising applications in materials science, urban planning, and precision agriculture, helping design solutions that conserve resources, support sustainability, and respond to real-time data in ways that classical computing cannot match.

Looking ahead, the future of quantum computing will focus on improvements in qubit technology and hybrid systems. Researchers are working to create more stable qubits, such as topological qubits, which may resist errors more effectively, along with more powerful quantum processors. Progress in error correction and coherence times aims to make quantum computers both practical and scalable, moving us closer to a future where they impact a broad range of industries.

The timeline we discussed outlines a likely path for quantum computing's growth over the coming years. In the current experimental phase (0-5 years), quantum systems with around 50-100 qubits are available through platforms like IBM Quantum Platform and Amazon Braket. Research focuses on foundational topics like algorithms, qubit stability, and error correction, with initial applications beginning to appear. These early applications may be modest, but they offer a preview of how quantum computing could support real-world needs.

In the early commercialization phase (5-10 years), quantum systems are expected to reach hundreds of qubits with greater stability, leading to specialized applications in multiple fields. This phase could see quantum-AI collaborations that enhance predictive models, optimize supply chains, and support molecular simulations in drug discovery. It's the beginning of quantum's transition from an experimental tool to a valuable asset in targeted fields.

As quantum computing moves into the widespread integration phase (10-15 years), hybrid quantum-classical systems may become standard in domains that rely on large datasets and advanced simulations, including climate science, pharmaceuticals, and cybersecurity. Quantum's ability to accelerate complex simulations and optimize resource-intensive processes may make it essential for areas like personalized healthcare, climate modeling, and secure digital communications, where high computational power is vital for accuracy and reliability.

In the mature systems phase (15-20+ years), fully reliable quantum computers may enable advances beyond just computation. Quantum cryptography could provide additional levels of security, while personalized medicine might benefit from treatments tailored at the molecular level. Quantum-driven sustainability models could optimize resource management, supporting more resilient environmental practices. Quantum computing may also support new discoveries in neurology, offering insights into the brain and enabling advancements in Brain-Machine Interfaces (BMIs) and space exploration. BMIs might use quantum systems for complex cognitive processing and secure communication, and space exploration could apply quantum precision in autonomous decision-making for sustainable interplanetary missions.

With quantum computing, we are on the edge of a new frontier, much like Captain Kirk and his crew in Star Trek. Just as the Enterprise ventured into uncharted regions of space, quantum computing allows us to explore entirely new realms of technology and knowledge. This technology could address challenges we once thought impossible to solve; a future where, like Starfleet's mission, we use advanced tools to improve life across diverse areas.

For those interested in quantum computing, now is an ideal time to explore the field. Platforms like Qiskit, Cirq, and Amazon Braket make it possible to experiment with quantum circuits and learn the fundamentals, regardless of technical background. Exploring quantum doesn't require expertise in physics, the field benefits from diverse skills, including software development, AI, ethics, and policy.

Whatever your interests, there is likely a role for you in this fast-moving field. Whether you build relevant skills or simply stay informed, you can be part of quantum technology's progress and its impact on society. As the field develops, our understanding of its potential will expand, and its role in everyday life will become more significant. The combination of quantum computing and AI brings new possibilities, with applications emerging across nearly every industry.

With quantum computing, we are entering a new era, one filled with opportunities to solve pressing issues and make significant advances. This field is still in its early stages, yet its potential to change the world is substantial. From improving environmental resilience to advancing personalized medicine and securing digital communications, quantum computing opens the door to a future where computation helps address some of the most intricate problems we face. Whether you're inspired to get involved or curious to observe, this field offers a future rich in discovery and potential.

APPENDICES

Part IV

Appendix A: Essential tools and techniques in quantum programming

For readers with a background in programming or an interest in diving deeper, this appendix introduces some foundational tools and techniques for working with quantum algorithms. While quantum computing requires a shift in how we approach programming, it's surprisingly accessible thanks to modern libraries and cloud-based quantum computing platforms. Here, you'll find an overview of some core quantum algorithms, practical resources, and toolkits like Qiskit, Cirq, and Amazon Braket, all of which make it possible to begin experimenting with quantum programming in Python.

Whether you're an experienced developer curious about the next frontier in computing or simply interested in seeing quantum mechanics in action, this section provides a starting point. You'll get a chance to explore:

- Core Quantum Algorithms like Shor's algorithm and **Grover's algorithm**, which showcase the power of quantum computing.

- Programming Tools and Libraries including IBM's Qiskit, Google's Cirq, and Amazon Braket, offering practical ways to create and test quantum circuits.

- Quantum Simulators that allow you to test quantum programs on your laptop before running them on actual quantum hardware.

By the end of this appendix, you'll have a foundational understanding of quantum programming essentials and a few practical examples to try on your own.

The TL;DR is that quantum programming differs from classical programming because it requires working with principles like superposition and quantum entanglement. But don't worry, anyone can learn it, thanks to the libraries, SDKs, and tools available today, many of which use plain Python. Major cloud providers now offer "Quantum-as-a-Service", allowing users to experiment on real quantum hardware through platforms like Amazon Braket, Microsoft Azure Quantum, and Google's Cirq. In addition, there are simulators available; that let you develop and test quantum algorithms directly on your laptop. These simulators make it easier to get hands-on experience and refine your code before running it on actual quantum hardware.

One of the best ways to understand quantum programming is to explore two of the most well-known quantum algorithms: Shor's algorithm and Grover's algorithm. Each of these algorithms shows how quantum computing can solve specific problems that are difficult or time-consuming for classical computers.

Shor's algorithm: A game-changer for cryptography

One of the most famous quantum algorithms, Shor's algorithm, can factor large numbers quickly. In classical computing, factoring large numbers is a difficult task; it takes classical computers so long that it forms the basis for many encryption systems, like RSA. Shor's algorithm, however, can factor these large numbers in a fraction of the time.

To understand why this matters, consider that many current security systems, like online banking encryption, rely on the difficulty of factoring large numbers to keep data safe. If a quantum computer can factor these numbers quickly, it could break traditional encryption methods, which is why there's a push for "quantum-safe" encryption as quantum computers develop. Shor's algorithm has proven the power of quantum computing in **cryptography** and continues to be one of its most talked-about breakthroughs.

Grover's algorithm: Speeding up data search

Another important quantum algorithm is Grover's algorithm, which speeds up the search process in large datasets. Classically, if you need to find an item in an unsorted list, you have to check each item one by one, which can take a long time. Grover's algorithm, however, allows a quantum computer to search the list much faster, with only about the square root of the total number of items.

For example, if you have a list of 1,000 items, a classical search might take, on average, 500 steps. With Grover's algorithm, a quantum computer could find the target in just 31 steps. This algorithm is useful for any situation where quick searching is needed, such as data retrieval, pattern recognition, or even in fields like drug discovery, where searching through molecular databases quickly can save significant time.

Designing simple quantum algorithms

Creating quantum algorithms can seem complex, but some basic examples can show the principles without needing a deep background in quantum mechanics. Let's walk through a simple quantum algorithm example you could try on a simulator.

Example: The quantum coin flip

One of the simplest examples of a quantum algorithm is a "quantum coin flip", which shows the concept of superposition. Consider a classical coin flip where you have heads or tails (0 or

1) with a 50% chance of either outcome. In a quantum coin flip, however, a qubit can exist in a state where it's both heads and tails at once, thanks to superposition.

1. **Start with a qubit in the |0⟩ state:** In quantum computing, |0⟩ represents the starting state (and is known as the zero state). Think of this as setting up a "heads" state.
2. **Apply the Hadamard gate:** This is like flipping the coin. The Hadamard gate puts the qubit into a superposition of |0⟩ (heads) and |1⟩ (tails), meaning it's equally likely to be measured as either.
3. **Measure the outcome:** When you measure the qubit, it will "collapse" to either |0⟩ or |1⟩, much like a coin flip landing on heads or tails.

By running this experiment multiple times, you should get a roughly even split of 0s and 1s, showing the concept of superposition in action. You can try this with a simple quantum circuit using libraries like Qiskit, which we'll cover in more detail below.

Example: The qubit flip error correction

Qubits are prone to errors because of their delicate nature, so error correction is important in quantum computing. A simple way to illustrate quantum error correction is with a "bit flip code", a technique that helps a quantum computer detect and correct basic errors.

1. **Start:** Start with a qubit in the **|0⟩** state.

2. **Duplicate the qubit state:** In classical computing, we could copy classical bits to check for errors, but in quantum computing, we use quantum entanglement to link qubits together instead. Here, we create two additional qubits and entangle them with the original qubit.
3. **Introduce an error:** Suppose one of the qubits flips accidentally because of interference ($|0\rangle$ becomes $|1\rangle$). By measuring all three qubits, we can check if an error occurred because the entangled state will show inconsistencies.
4. **Correct the error:** If the original qubit's state differs from the entangled pair, we know an error happened and can correct it by flipping the qubit back.

This process shows how quantum error correction works on a basic level and is fundamental for more complex quantum algorithms.

Toolkits and libraries for quantum computing

Several Python-based toolkits and libraries make experimenting with quantum algorithms easier than ever, offering tools to create, simulate, and even run quantum circuits on actual quantum hardware. Here's a guide to some of the most popular options:

- **Qiskit (IBM):** Developed by IBM, Qiskit is a powerful open-source quantum computing framework that supports building and running quantum circuits, experimenting with various algorithms, and accessing

IBM's quantum hardware. Qiskit also provides simulators, making it a fantastic choice for beginners and professionals alike.

Example: With Qiskit's built-in simulator, you can experiment with concepts like the quantum coin flip or Grover's algorithm, running tests directly on your laptop. For those looking to go further, Qiskit integrates with IBM's Quantum Experience cloud, where you can execute your algorithms on real quantum processors like the IBM Eagle. Picture testing Shor's algorithm to factorize numbers on a real quantum machine, a step that brings theoretical concepts to life.

- **Cirq (Google):** Cirq is Google's quantum computing library for designing, simulating, and running quantum circuits, especially for **noisy intermediate-scale quantum (NISQ)** computers – the types of quantum computers currently available, that work well for smaller, experimental tasks. Cirq provides extensive control over each gate and qubit interaction, making it ideal for advanced users who want flexibility in building custom algorithms.

Example: With Cirq, you can test out error correction techniques, like the bit-flip error correction we discussed, to see how interference affects quantum circuits. You could also connect Cirq to Google's Sycamore processor via Google's cloud platform to run experiments on real quantum hardware, exploring quantum supremacy concepts and seeing firsthand how different algorithms handle large-scale data.

- **Braket SDK (AWS):** Amazon Braket offers a managed quantum computing service on AWS, providing access to quantum processors from various providers, including IonQ, Rigetti, and D-Wave. Braket's SDK integrates smoothly with AWS services, making it especially useful for those already familiar with the AWS ecosystem. Braket also includes robust simulators that let you test algorithms before running them on actual quantum hardware, allowing for a seamless development experience.

Example: With Amazon Braket, you can experiment on IonQ's trapped-ion quantum processors or Rigetti's superconducting processors, each suited to different types of algorithms. For instance, IonQ's qubits, made from trapped ions, are particularly stable, making them ideal for precision-based algorithms like Grover's search algorithm. If you're developing algorithms that demand high stability, experimenting on IonQ's hardware could provide unique insights. Additionally, Braket offers simulated annealing on D-Wave's quantum annealers, making it suitable for optimization problems in logistics or machine learning.

- **Azure Quantum (Microsoft):** Microsoft's Azure Quantum offers a hybrid approach, combining classical and quantum computing resources in the cloud. Azure

Quantum provides access to multiple types of quantum processors, including those from IonQ and Honeywell, and integrates with Q#, Microsoft's own quantum programming language.

Example: With Azure Quantum, you can run optimization algorithms across classical and quantum hardware, making it a great choice for complex simulations. For instance, you could experiment with portfolio optimization on Honeywell's trapped-ion processors or test quantum error correction methods on IonQ's processors. Azure Quantum's hybrid nature also means that you can use classical computing resources alongside quantum processing, offering a bridge between traditional computing and quantum advancements.

These toolkits provide accessible paths to learning quantum programming, making it easier to experiment and build quantum algorithms right from your laptop. Each platform's simulators let you test and refine algorithms before running them on real quantum hardware.

The hardware options vary across platforms, generally offering anywhere from tens to over a hundred qubits, depending on the provider. Simulators allow for flexible experimentation with similar or higher qubit counts, enabling you to work with quantum algorithms without needing access to physical quantum devices.

So, whether you're exploring a basic quantum coin flip or working on complex cryptography problems, these libraries allow you to experiment with cutting-edge technology from wherever you are.

Appendix B: Foundations of quantum machine learning (QML)

Quantum Machine Learning is an interdisciplinary field that applies quantum computing to classical machine learning tasks. At its core, QML leverages the principles of quantum mechanics (superposition, quantum entanglement, and interference) to process data more efficiently than classical approaches. Unlike traditional ML, which operates on classical bits, QML operates on qubits. Qubits, thanks to superposition, can represent both 0 and 1 simultaneously, allowing QML algorithms to explore a much larger solution space in parallel, which offers significant speedup potential for complex, data-intensive tasks.

Quantum computation, particularly with gate-based quantum computers, involves applying quantum gates (analogous to classical logic gates) to qubits. These gates manipulate qubits to represent and process information in ways that exploit quantum superposition and quantum entanglement. When applied to ML, quantum gates can represent high-dimensional transformations that map data into feature spaces beyond the reach of classical computers, providing alternative approaches for tasks such as clustering, classification, and dimensionality reduction.

Key components of quantum machine learning

Quantum states and data encoding

Encoding classical data into quantum states is a fundamental aspect of QML. Two common methods for encoding data include amplitude encoding, where data is encoded directly in the amplitudes of a quantum state, and angle encoding, where data features are represented as rotation angles of qubits.

For instance, when we need to encode a classical dataset with many elements, amplitude encoding can represent this data in a quantum state, effectively compressing the information into a much smaller quantum space. However, this encoding process is challenging and computationally intensive, making it one of the key bottlenecks in Quantum Machine Learning (QML).

Quantum circuits for machine learning

- QML algorithms use quantum circuits designed to manipulate qubits in ways that achieve specific ML tasks. A common framework is the parametrized quantum circuit (PQC), which applies a series of quantum gates with adjustable parameters.

- These parameters are trained, similar to weights in a neural network, using classical optimization algorithms to minimize a predefined cost function. Hybrid quantum-classical approaches are common, where a quantum processor executes the quantum circuit and a classical processor performs the optimization, typically using gradient-based methods.

- An example is the Variational Quantum Classifier (VQC), a quantum analog to a classical linear classifier that uses a parametrized quantum circuit to generate a decision boundary for classification tasks.

Quantum kernels and quantum feature spaces

- Quantum kernels leverage quantum states to represent complex feature spaces that classical methods cannot efficiently explore. By mapping data points into high-dimensional Hilbert spaces, quantum kernels allow QML models to learn non-linear patterns that may be challenging for classical models.

- In kernel-based QML, we compute inner products in a quantum Hilbert space, leveraging quantum mechanics to evaluate the similarity between data points. The quantum feature space can be explored via the Quantum Kernel Estimation (QKE) algorithm, which has shown advantages in pattern recognition tasks where data has an inherent quantum structure.

Quantum speedup in QML

- Quantum algorithms like the Quantum Phase Estimation and Quantum Fourier Transform allow certain ML tasks to be computed more efficiently than with classical algorithms. For instance, the Harrow-Hassidim-Lloyd (HHL) algorithm for linear systems offers a quantum speedup for solving linear equations, which can be utilized in various ML techniques like regression and support vector machines.

- For data processing tasks, such as principal component analysis (PCA) or clustering, quantum algorithms can expedite computation by leveraging superposition to perform many operations concurrently. However, speedups are conditional and depend heavily on data encoding efficiency and quantum hardware constraints.

Applications of QML

Quantum neural networks (QNNs)

- Quantum Neural Networks are an extension of classical neural networks where quantum circuits serve as "quantum neurons". Each layer of a QNN applies quantum gates to perform operations analogous to weighted sums and activation functions in classical neural networks.

- Training QNNs involves a hybrid quantum-classical approach, where quantum circuits are used to evaluate the network's forward pass, and a classical optimizer adjusts parameters based on a cost function. The non-linear nature of quantum circuits makes QNNs highly expressive and suitable for pattern recognition tasks.

Quantum-enhanced reinforcement learning (QRL)

- In reinforcement learning, quantum computation can enhance policy learning by enabling faster sampling and more efficient state exploration. Quantum algorithms, such as Grover's search algorithm have been adapted for QRL to accelerate the exploration of large action spaces, enabling faster convergence to optimal policies.

- QRL is promising for environments with complex, high-dimensional state spaces, where classical methods struggle with exploration-exploitation trade-offs. In QRL, quantum circuits can approximate complex action-value functions, providing potential speedups in learning optimal strategies for tasks like robotics or autonomous navigation.

Quantum support vector machines (QSVMs)

- Support Vector Machines (SVMs) are a fundamental classification tool, and their quantum extension, QSVM, leverages quantum kernel methods to classify data points. By using quantum circuits to compute kernel values, QSVMs can operate in high-dimensional spaces, making them particularly effective for tasks with non-linearly separable data.

- QSVMs have been applied in fields such as image recognition, financial modeling, and bioinformatics, where high-dimensional pattern recognition is crucial. Quantum kernels help SVMs generalize to more complex data structures, potentially outperforming classical SVMs.

Real-world QML initiatives and research

- **IBM's Quantum Open Science:** IBM has released QML toolkits and conducted research that applies quantum circuits to optimize models for fraud detection and supply chain logistics. IBM's Qiskit provides access to quantum libraries for building QML models, allowing researchers to implement and test QSVMs, quantum classifiers, and kernel estimations.

- **Google's Quantum TensorFlow:** Google has integrated quantum components into TensorFlow, allowing researchers to create hybrid quantum-classical machine learning models. Google's Quantum AI team has focused on exploring quantum neural networks and their applications in image recognition and natural language processing.

- **Xanadu's PennyLane:** Xanadu's open-source PennyLane platform enables the development of QML algorithms using differentiable quantum circuits. Xanadu is leading advancements in quantum neural networks (QNNs) and has applied quantum machine learning (QML) to model complex quantum chemistry simulations, with potential benefits for drug discovery and materials science.

Limitations and future directions in QML

While QML offers exciting prospects, it faces several limitations:

- **Hardware constraints:** Current quantum hardware is limited in qubit count, coherence time, and gate fidelity. These limitations restrict the complexity and depth of QML models that can be executed, particularly for large-scale datasets.

- **Data loading and encoding challenges:** Efficiently encoding classical data into quantum states is challenging. Methods like amplitude encoding require preprocessing and significant computational resources, limiting the scalability of QML for large datasets. Research in developing efficient quantum data encodings is ongoing.

- **Algorithmic scalability:** QML's promise of speedup is conditional on factors such as quantum hardware capability and specific algorithmic requirements. Many QML algorithms, while theoretically advantageous, face implementation challenges that limit their real-world applicability until larger, more stable quantum processors become available.

- **Optimization and training challenges:** Quantum models often rely on classical optimizers to train parametrized circuits, a process prone to challenges like barren plateaus, where gradients vanish, stalling the training process. Advanced optimization techniques, including gradient-free methods and reinforcement learning, are being explored to overcome these issues.

The road ahead for QML

As quantum technology advances, QML is expected to unlock capabilities that redefine computational approaches in machine learning:

- **Quantum-assisted neural networks:** Quantum processors could aid in training deep neural networks by accelerating matrix operations and reducing training times. For AI models in fields like image processing, quantum-enhanced neural networks may enable models that can learn from more complex patterns.

- **Improved quantum algorithms for ML:** Ongoing research into quantum gradient estimation and variational quantum algorithms aims to improve the stability and scalability of QML. These innovations could make QML applicable to real-world problems in natural language processing, genomics, and autonomous systems.

- **Hybrid quantum-classical models:** The near-term future of QML is likely hybrid, where quantum processors handle the computationally intensive parts of ML tasks while classical processors manage data pre-processing and optimization. As hybrid models mature, they could enable faster, more scalable applications in multiple fields.

Appendix C: References

1. Shankar, R. Principles of Quantum Mechanics. Yale University Press, 1994.
2. Susskind, Leonard, and Friedman, Art. Quantum Mechanics: The Theoretical Minimum. Basic Books, 2015.
3. "Quantum Mechanics". Stanford Encyclopedia of Philosophy. https://plato.stanford.edu/entries/qm/
4. "Quantum Mechanics". Khan Academy. https://www.khanacademy.org/science/physics/quantum-physics
5. Kumar, Manjit. Quantum: Einstein, Bohr, and the Great Debate about the Nature of Reality. Icon Books, 2010.
6. Farmelo, Graham. The Strangest Man: The Hidden Life of Paul Dirac, Mystic of the Atom. Faber & Faber, 2011.
7. Nielsen, Michael A., and Chuang, Isaac L. Quantum Computation and Quantum Information; 10th Anniversary Edition. Cambridge University Press, 2010.
8. Kaye, Phillip, Laflamme, Raymond, and Mosca, Michele. An Introduction to Quantum Computing. Oxford University Press, 2007.
9. "Quantum Computing". IBM Quantum Platform. https://quantum-computing.ibm.com
10. Yanofsky, Noson S., and Mannucci, Mirco A. Quantum Computing for Computer Scientists. Cambridge University Press, 2008.
11. Quantum Computing: Progress and Prospects. National Academies of Sciences, Engineering, and Medicine, 2019. https://nap.nationalacademies.org/catalog/25196/quantum-computing-progress-and-prospects

12. Johnston, Eric R., Harrigan, Nic, and Gimeno-Segovia, Mercedes. Programming Quantum Computers: Essential Algorithms and Code Samples. O'Reilly Media, 2019.
13. "Quantum Machine Learning". Wikipedia. https://en.wikipedia.org/wiki/Quantum_machine_learning
14. "Qiskit Documentation". Qiskit.org. https://qiskit.org/documentation/
15. "TensorFlow Quantum". TensorFlow.org. https://www.tensorflow.org/quantum
16. "CERN Quantum Technology Initiative". CERN. https://quantum.cern
17. "WACQT at Chalmers University". Chalmers University. https://www.chalmers.se/en/centres/wacqt
18. "UK National Quantum Computing Centre to house 12 quantum computers". Computing.co.uk. https://www.computing.co.uk/news/2024/uk-national-quantum-computing-centre-house-12-quantum-computers
19. "Project QSolid: Quantum computer demonstrator in operation". ScienceX. https://sciencex.com/wire-news/492779663/project-qsolid-quantum-computer-demonstrator-in-operation.html
20. "Google Quantum AI". Google. https://quantumai.google
21. "IBM Quantum Computing". IBM Research. https://research.ibm.com/quantum-computing
22. "List of Open Quantum Projects". Quantum Open Source Foundation (QOSF). https://qosf.org/project_list/
23. "Xiong'an New Area Official Website". Xiong'an. http://www.xiongan.gov.cn
24. "NDRC Official Website". National Development and Reform

Commission (NDRC).
https://en.ndrc.gov.cn

25. "China's Quantum Leap: Xiong'an as a Technological Hub". South China Morning Post. https://www.scmp.com/tech/innovation/article/3123456/chinas-quantum-leap-xiongan-technological-hub
26. Miranda, Eduardo, et al. "Quantum Brain Networks: A Perspective". Electronics, 2022. https://www.mdpi.com/2079-9292/11/10/1528
27. Miranda, Eduardo Reck. "On Interfacing the Brain with Quantum Computers: An Approach to Listen to the Logic of the Mind". Quantum Computing in the Arts and Humanities, 2021. https://arxiv.org/abs/2101.03887
28. "Quantum-Based Agriculture: The Final Frontier". Coventry University. https://pure.coventry.ac.uk/ws/portalfiles/portal/13286036/quantumcomb.pdf
29. "Quantum Computing and Space Exploration: Unleashing the Potential of Topological Quantum Computing". Medium, 2023. https://medium.com/%40EmilyD56/quantum-computing-and-space-exploration-unleashing-the-potential-of-topological-quantum-computing-e28f11ebcd63
30. "Microsoft Wants to Build a Quantum Supercomputer Within a Decade" SingularityHub 2023, https://singularityhub.com/2023/07/05/microsoft-plans-to-build-a-quantum-supercomputer-within-a-decade/
31. "Quantum Technologies in Space". Experimental Astronomy, 2021. https://link.springer.com/article/10.1007/s10686-021-09731-x
32. "Test Quantum Mechanics in Space – Invest US$1 Billion". Nature, 2021. https://www.nature.com/articles/d41586-021-02091-8
33. "What is Quantum Computing?" NASA. https://www.nasa.gov/technology/computing/what-is-quantum-computing

34. "Space Station to Host 'Self-Healing' Quantum Communications Tech Demo". NASA Jet Propulsion Laboratory. https://www.jpl.nasa.gov/news/space-station-to-host-self-healing-quantum-communications-tech-demo
35. "Quantum Computing for Modelling Climate". University of Southern Denmark. https://www.sdu.dk/en/forskning/qm/quantum-computing/qc-climate-modeling
36. Cartier, Kimberly M. S. "How Quantum Computing Can Tackle Climate and Energy Challenges". Eos, 2022. https://eos.org/features/how-quantum-computing-can-tackle-climate-and-energy-challenges
37. "Quantum Technology, a Pivotal Resource in Climate Change Mitigation". IEEE Climate Change. https://climate-change.ieee.org/news/quantum-technology/
38. Egger, Daniel J., Gambella, Claudio, et al. "Quantum Computing for Finance: State-of-the-Art and Future Prospects". IEEE Transactions on Quantum Engineering, 2020. https://ieeexplore.ieee.org/document/9222275
39. "Exploring Quantum Computing Use Cases for Logistics". IBM Institute for Business Value. https://www.ibm.com/thought-leadership/institute-business-value/en-us/report/quantum-logistics
40. "Quantum Computing in Logistics: Optimizing Supply Chains". Quantum Zeitgeist. https://quantumzeitgeist.com/quantum-computing-in-logistics-optimizing-supply-chains/
41. "Quantum Routes: How Quantum Computing is Set to Revolutionize Navigation and Optimization in Logistics". Fast Company. https://www.fastcompany.com/90976690/quantum-routes-how-quantum-computing-is-set-to-revolutionize-navigation-and-optimization-in-logistics

42. "How Quantum Computing Could Help Optimize Logistics". The Wall Street Journal. https://www.wsj.com/podcasts/tech-news-briefing/how-quantum-computing-could-help-optimize-logistics/8DF7305E-F3DB-4F7D-A161-E184B53ED84F
43. Castelvecchi, Davide. "The AI–Quantum Computing Mash-up: Will It Revolutionize Science?" Nature, January 2, 2024. https://www.nature.com/articles/d41586-023-04007-0
44. "In-Depth Guide to Quantum Artificial Intelligence". AIMultiple, October 2024. https://research.aimultiple.com/quantum-ai/
45. "Quantum Computing and AI". KI - Künstliche Intelligenz, October 2024. https://link.springer.com/article/10.1007/s13218-024-00872-7
46. "Artificial Intelligence and Machine Learning for Quantum Technologies". Physical Review A, January 2023. https://link.aps.org/doi/10.1103/PhysRevA.107.010101
47. "Artificial Intelligence Computing at the Quantum Level". MDPI, March 2022. https://www.mdpi.com/2306-5729/7/3/28
48. "Pioneers of Revolutionary CRISPR Gene Editing Win Chemistry Nobel". Nature, October 7, 2020. https://www.nature.com/articles/d41586-020-02765-9
49. "Gensaxen CRISPR-Cas9 Revolutionerar Gentekniken". Umeå Universitet. https://www.umu.se/forskning/var-forskning/fordjupa-dig/gensaxen-crispr-cas9-revolutionerar-gentekniken/
50. "Scientists Use Quantum Biology, AI to Sharpen Genome Editing Tool". Oak Ridge National Laboratory. https://www.ornl.gov/news/scientists-use-quantum-biology-ai-sharpen-genome-editing-tool
51. "Quantum Biological Insights into CRISPR-Cas9 sgRNA Efficiency from Explainable Machine Learning". Nucleic Acids Research, October 2023. https://academic.oup.com/nar/article/51/19/10147/7279034

52. "About Xanadu". Xanadu Quantum Computing. https://www.xanadu.ai/about/
53. "Xanadu Launches First Public Cloud-Deployed Computer with Quantum Computational Advantage". PR Newswire, June 2022. https://www.prnewswire.com/news-releases/xanadu-launches-first-public-cloud-deployed-computer-with-quantum-computational-advantage-301559097.html
54. "Quantum Computing at BASF". BASF. https://www.basf.com/global/en/who-we-are/innovation/how-we-innovate/our-RnD/Digitalization_in_R-D/quantum_computing.html
55. "Materials Science Applications for Quantum Computing on the QUCUN Platform: HQS Receives an Order from BASF". HQS Quantum Simulations. https://quantumsimulations.de/news/materials-science-applications-for-quantum-computing-on-the-qucun-platform-hqs-receives-an-order-from-basf
56. "Amazon Braket Overview". Amazon Web Services. https://aws.amazon.com/braket/
57. "Company Overview". IonQ. https://ionq.com/
58. "IonQ Achieves Industry-Leading Performance on Next-Generation Barium Qubits". IonQ Investors News. https://investors.ionq.com/news/news-details/2023/IonQ-Achieves-Industry-Leading-Performance-on-Next-Generation-Barium-Qubits/default.aspx
59. "Company Website". AstraZeneca. https://www.astrazeneca.com/
60. "Company Overview". Qubit Pharmaceuticals. https://www.qubit-pharmaceuticals.com/
61. "Company Website". Quantinuum. https://www.quantinuum.com/
62. "NASA's Quantum AI Lab". NASA. https://www.nasa.gov/

intelligent-systems-division/discovery-and-systems-health/nasa-quail/

63. "Company Overview". TerraPower. https://terrapower.com/
64. "Company Website". NuScale Power. https://www.nuscalepower.com/
65. "Quantum Computing Research". JPMorgan Chase. https://www.jpmorgan.com/technology/applied-research
66. "Company Overview". Rigetti Computing. https://www.rigetti.com/
67. "Company Website". Citadel. https://www.citadel.com/
68. "Company Overview". D-Wave. https://www.dwavesys.com/
69. "Company Website". OTI Lumionics. https://www.otilumionics.com/
70. "Engineering Quantum Algorithms". Goldman Sachs. https://www.goldmansachs.com/careers/blog/possibilities-quantum-computing
71. "Can Europe beat China and the US in quantum computing?" Goldman Sachs, https://www.goldmansachs.com/insights/articles/can-europe-beat-china-and-the-us-in-quantum-computing
72. "Quantum Computing". Volkswagen Group. https://www.vw.com/en/newsroom/future-of-mobility/quantum-computing.html
73. "Quantum Information Science". NIST. https://www.nist.gov/quantum-information-science
74. "China Reaches New Milestone in Space-Based Quantum Communications". SciAm, 2020. https://www.scientificamerican.com/article/china-reaches-new-milestone-in-space-based-quantum-communications/

75. "Organization Overview". Ethereum Foundation. https://ethereum.org/en/foundation/
76. "Smart Nation Singapore". Government of Singapore. https://www.smartnation.gov.sg/
77. "Company Overview". Blackrock Neurotech. https://blackrockneurotech.com/
78. "EU Artificial Intelligence Act". European Commission. https://artificialintelligenceact.eu/
79. "See & Spray". John Deere. https://www.deere.com/en/sprayers/see-spray-ultimate/
80. "FieldView". Bayer. https://www.cropscience.bayer.us/tools/fieldview
81. "World Agri-Tech 2024: Pioneering agriculture resilience with AI". Microsoft. https://www.microsoft.com/en-us/industry/blog/sustainability/2024/04/02/world-agri-tech-2024-pioneering-agriculture-resilience-with-ai/
82. "Harnessing quantum computing for smart agriculture: Empowering sustainable crop management and yield optimization". ScienceDirect, https://www.sciencedirect.com/science/article/abs/pii/S0168169924000711
83. "Quantum Sensing for Precision Agriculture: Google's Role in Feeding the Future". IT Fix, November 2024 https://itfix.org.uk/quantum-sensing-for-precision-agriculture-googles-role-in-feeding-the-future/
84. "Quantum Quants and TNO: Electrical Grid Optimization Powered by Quantum Computing" D-Wave Systems. https://www.dwavesys.com/media/5q3l3uno/tnoqq_electrical-grid-optimization_case_study_2-0.pdf
85. "Company Overview". Neuralink. https://neuralink.com/

86. "Company Overview". Synchron. https://synchron.com/
87. "Synchron's Stentrode Neural Interface". MIT Technology Review. https://www.technologyreview.com/2024/04/19/1091505/companies-brain-computer-interfaces/
88. "Meta's Reality Labs: Brain-Machine Interface Innovation". Meta. https://about.facebook.com/realitylabs
89. "Brain-Machine Interfaces and Neuralink: Privacy and Ethical Concerns". Berkeley School of Information Blog. https://blogs.ischool.berkeley.edu/w231/2021/07/09/brain-machine-interfaces-and-neuralink-privacy-and-ethical-concerns/
90. "Human Brain Connected Wirelessly to Computer for First Time". Blackrock Neurotech Insights. https://blackrockneurotech.com/insights/human-brain-connected-wirelessly-to-computer-for-first-time-ever/
91. "Neural Lace and Brain-Computer Interface Advances". Blackrock Neurotech Insights. https://blackrockneurotech.com/insights/nueralace-bci-interface/
92. "Quantum and Neural Interface Research". Nature. https://www.nature.com/articles/d41586-024-00304-4
93. "Broad Institute and Verily Partner with Microsoft to Accelerate the Next Generation of the Terra Platform for Health and Life Science Research". Microsoft News, January 2021. https://news.microsoft.com/2021/01/11/broad-institute-and-verily-partner-with-microsoft-to-accelerate-the-next-generation-of-the-terra-platform-for-health-and-life-science-research/
94. "Researchers Flip Genes On and Off with AI-Designed DNA Switches". The Jackson Laboratory, 2024. https://www.jax.org/news-and-insights/2024/october/researchers-flip-genes-on-and-off-with-ai-designed-dna-switches

95. "QuEra Computing Inc". Wikipedia. https://en.wikipedia.org/wiki/QuEra_Computing_Inc.
96. "MIT's BioAutoMATED: An Open-Source Machine-Learning Platform for Research Labs". MIT News, 2023. https://news.mit.edu/2023/bioautomated-open-source-machine-learning-platform-for-research-labs-0706
97. "How One Lab Uses Machine Learning to Solve a Key Gene Therapy Problem". Broad Institute. https://www.broadinstitute.org/news/how-one-lab-uses-machine-learning-solve-key-gene-therapy-problem
98. "Qubit Pharmaceuticals and Institut Curie Partner on Cancer Drug Development", Institut Curie. 2023. https://presse.curie.fr/calcul-haute-performance-simulation-et-ia-qubit-pharmaceuticals-linstitut-curie-et-luniversite-de-bordeaux-sassocient-pour-accelerer-le-developpement-de-voies-therapeutiques-inedit/
99. "Qubit Pharmaceuticals Leverages NVIDIA for Hybrid Quantum Computing in Drug Discovery". Actu IA, 2023. https://www.actuia.com/english/qubit-pharmaceuticals-leverages-nvidia-and-hybrid-quantum-computing-to-accelerate-drug-discovery/
100. "Pfizer and IBM Partner to Improve Clinical Trials with Generative AI and Quantum Computing". Nature biotechnology, 2023. https://www.nature.com/articles/s41587-024-02251-x.pdf
101. "Accenture Labs and 1QBit Work with Biogen to Apply Quantum Computing to Accelerate Drug Discovery". 1QBit, 2017. https://1qbit.com/news/accenture-labs-1qbit-work-biogen-apply-quantum-computing-accelerate-drug-discovery/
102. "Qubit Pharmaceuticals Accelerates Drug Discovery With Hybrid Quantum Computing". NVIDIA, 2022. https://blogs.nvidia.com/blog/qubit-pharmaceuticals-accelerates-

drug-discovery-quantum-computing/

103. "Quantum Computing". NVIDIA. https://www.nvidia.com/en-us/solutions/quantum-computing/

104. "DeepMind's AI predicts almost exactly when and where it's going to rain". MIT Technology Review, 2021. https://www.technologyreview.com/2021/09/29/1036331/deepminds-ai-predicts-almost-exactly-when-and-where-its-going-to-rain/

105. "DeepMind and the UK Met Office collaborate to improve weather forecasting". InfoQ, 2021. https://www.infoq.com/news/2021/12/deepmind-weather-forecasting/

106. "Towards Quantum Ocean Modelling: Quantum Annealing for Ocean Dynamics". arXiv, 2023. https://arxiv.org/abs/2405.11782

107. "IBM Deep Thunder". Wikipedia, 2023. https://en.wikipedia.org/wiki/IBM_Deep_Thunder

108. "NRC certifies first U.S. small modular reactor design". U.S. Department of Energy, 2023. https://www.energy.gov/ne/articles/nrc-certifies-first-us-small-modular-reactor-design

109. "Funding secured to enable small modular reactor delivery to meet net zero". Rolls-Royce SMR, 2023. https://www.rolls-royce-smr.com/press/funding-secured-to-enable-small-modular-reactor-delivery-to-meet-net-zero

110. "Perovskite solar cell". Wikipedia, 2023. https://en.wikipedia.org/wiki/Perovskite_solar_cell

111. "Thin-film solar cell". Wikipedia, 2023. https://en.wikipedia.org/wiki/Thin-film_solar_cell

112. "BGS to help further CO_2 monitoring research at Sutton Bonington". British Geological Survey, 2023. https://www.bgs.ac.uk/news/bgs-to-help-further-co2-monitoring-

research-at-sutton-bonington/

113. "UK National Quantum Technologies Programme (NQTP)". UK Research and Innovation, 2023. https://uknqt.ukri.org/
114. "BMW Group, Airbus, and Quantinuum collaborate to fast-track sustainable mobility research using cutting-edge quantum computers". Quantinuum, 2023. https://www.quantinuum.com/press-releases/bmw-group-airbus-and-quantinuum-collaborate-to-fast-track-sustainable-mobility-research-using-cutting-edge-quantum-computers
115. "Quantum technologies". Airbus, 2023. https://www.airbus.com/en/innovation/digital-transformation/quantum-technologies
116. "Rigetti Computing awarded Innovate UK grant to enhance quantum machine learning methods for anti-money laundering detection". GlobeNewswire, 2023. https://www.globenewswire.com/news-release/2023/11/01/2771203/0/en/Rigetti-Computing-Awarded-Innovate-UK-Grant-to-Enhance-Quantum-Machine-Learning-Methods-for-Anti-Money-Laundering-Detection.html
117. "Rigetti and Nasdaq team up to pursue quantum advantage in the financial industry". Rigetti Computing, 2022. https://investors.rigetti.com/news-releases/news-release-details/rigetti-and-nasdaq-team-pursue-quantum-advantage-financial
118. "Global Quantitative Strategies". Citadel, 2023. https://www.citadel.com/what-we-do/global-quantitative-strategies/
119. "IBM Quantum roadmap to 2025". IBM, 2023. https://www.ibm.com/quantum/blog/ibm-quantum-roadmap-2025
120. "Performance evaluation of quantum annealing for financial portfolio optimization". SpringerLink, 2021.

https://link.springer.com/chapter/10.1007/978-3-030-77980-1_4

121. "Portfolio optimization using quantum annealing". GitHub – D-Wave Examples, 2023. https://github.com/dwave-examples/portfolio-optimization
122. "OTI Lumionics: Materials discovery with D-Wave quantum annealers". D-Wave Quantum, 2022. https://dwavequantum.com/media/vpzj35s1/34_thurs_am_oti.pdf
123. "Quantum algorithms for derivatives pricing". Quantum Journal, 2021. https://quantum-journal.org/papers/q-2021-06-01-463/
124. "Quantum advantage for market risk computation". Quantum Journal, 2022. https://quantum-journal.org/papers/q-2022-07-20-770/
125. "Quantum computing for option pricing". Quantum Journal, 2020. https://quantum-journal.org/papers/q-2020-07-06-291/
126. "Standard Chartered and Universities Space Research Association join forces on quantum computing". Standard Chartered, 2020. https://www.sc.com/en/press-release/standard-chartered-and-universities-space-research-association-join-forces-on-quantum-computing/
127. "Standard Chartered Bank renews partnership with USRA for advanced machine learning applications". Inside Quantum Technology, 2022. https://www.insidequantumtechnology.com/news-archive/usra-standard-chartered-bank-renew-partnership-focus-on-machine-learning/
128. "SC Ventures explores quantum computing with USRA for data and AI solutions". SC Ventures, 2020. https://scventures.io/standard-chartered-and-universities-space-research-association-join-forces-on-quantum-computing/
129. "Terra Quantum and Volkswagen Data:Lab demonstrate hybrid quantum computing use cases". The Quantum Insider, 2022.

https://thequantuminsider.com/2022/05/12/terra-quantum-and-volkswagen-datalab-demonstrate-hybrid-quantum-computing-use-cases/

130. "Digital pioneering work: Volkswagen uses quantum computers for traffic flow optimization". Volkswagen Group, 2017. https://www.volkswagen-group.com/en/press-releases/digital-pioneering-work-volkswagen-uses-quantum-computers-16496
131. "Will Quantum Computers Create Value – and When?" Boston Consulting Group, 2019. https://www.bcg.com/publications/2019/quantum-computers-create-value-when
132. "What Happens When 'If' Turns to 'When' in Quantum Computing". Boston Consulting Group, 2021. https://web-assets.bcg.com/89/00/d2d074424a6ca820b1238e24ccc0/bcg-what-happens-when-if-turns-to-when-in-quantum-computing-jul-2021-r.pdf
133. "DHL launches latest DHL Logistics Trend Radar with most impactful trends". DHL, 2022. https://group.dhl.com/en/media-relations/press-releases/2022/dhl-launches-latest-dhl-logistics-trend-radar-with-most-impactful-trends.html
134. "DHL Logistics Trend Radar unveils emerging AI trends and sustainable solutions". DHL, 2024. https://group.dhl.com/en/media-relations/press-releases/2024/dhl-logistics-trend-radar-unveils-emerging-ai-trends-and-sustainable-solutions.html
135. "The science behind grouping package deliveries". Amazon Science, 2022. https://www.amazon.science/latest-news/the-science-behind-grouping-amazon-package-deliveries
136. "Where machine learning models meet mobility and human

behavior". Amazon Science, 2023. https://www.amazon.science/working-at-amazon/mahdieh-allahviranloo-last-mile-delivery-research

137. "AWS last mile solution for faster delivery, lower costs, and a better customer experience". AWS Supply Chain, 2023. https://aws.amazon.com/blogs/supply-chain/aws-last-mile-solution-for-faster-delivery-lower-costs-and-a-better-customer-experience/

138. "Raj Hazra, Quantinuum technology boss, to drive computing's quantum leap". The Times, 2021. https://www.thetimes.co.uk/article/raj-hazra-quantinuum-technology-boss-drive-computings-quantum-leap-3rl5s0038

139. "Cambridge Quantum merges with Honeywell Quantum Solutions to form Quantinuum". The Times, 2021. https://www.thetimes.co.uk/article/raj-hazra-quantinuum-technology-boss-drive-computings-quantum-leap-3rl5s0038

140. "Materials science applications for quantum computing on the QuCUN platform – HQS receives an order from BASF". HQS Quantum Simulations, 2022. https://quantumsimulations.de/news/materials-science-applications-for-quantum-computing-on-the-qucun-platform-hqs-receives-an-order-from-basf

141. "Bosch, BASF, HQS Quantum Simulations & institutes team up in MANIQU project to research novel materials on quantum computers". HQS Quantum Simulations, 2023. https://quantumsimulations.de/news/bosch-basf-hqs-quantum-simulations-institutes-team-up-in-maniqu-project-to-research-novel-materials-on-quantum-computers

142. "The best of both worlds: how to solve real problems on modern quantum computers". Argonne Leadership Computing Facility.

2019.
https://www.alcf.anl.gov/news/best-both-worlds-how-solve-real-problems-modern-quantum-computers

143. "Five cities pioneering digital twin technology". Build in Digital. https://buildindigital.com/five-cities-pioneering-digital-twin-technology/
144. "Boeing Pioneering Quantum Communications Technology with In-Space Test Satellite". Boeing. 2024. https://investors.boeing.com/investors/news/press-release-details/2024/Boeing-Pioneering-Quantum-Communications-Technology-with-In-Space-Test-Satellite/default.aspx
145. "Google and NASA Launch Quantum Computing AI Lab". MIT Technology Review. https://www.technologyreview.com/2013/05/16/253052/google-and-nasa-launch-quantum-computing-ai-lab/
146. "Brain Machine Interfaces Market By Type (Invasive, Partially, Non-invasive), By Application (Healthcare, Communication And Control, Gaming And Entertainment, Smart Home Controls, Military And Defense, Other End Users) - Growth, Future Prospects And Competitive Analysis, 2019 - 2027". Brisk Insights. https://www.briskinsights.com/report/brain-machine-interfaces-market
147. "Travelling salesman problem". Wikipedia, 2024. https://en.wikipedia.org/wiki/Travelling_salesman_problem
148. "Vehicle Routing Problem". Wikipedia, 2024. https://en.wikipedia.org/wiki/Vehicle_routing_problem
149. "Waymo puts the brakes on self-driving trucks program". TechCrunch, 2023. https://techcrunch.com/2023/07/26/waymo-puts-the-brakes-on-self-driving-trucks-program/
150. "Self-driving semi-trucks have already hit the road". NY Post, 2024.

https://nypost.com/2024/04/01/self-driving-semi-trucks-have-already-hit-the-road/[1]

151. "Quantum computing: the hype and hopes". ABB, 2024. https://new.abb.com/news/detail/74736/quantum-computing-the-hype-and-hopes
152. "Siemens collaborates with Pasqal to research quantum applications in computer-aided engineering, simulation, and testing". Pasqal, 2024. https://www.pasqal.com/news/siemens-collaborates-with-pasqal-to-research-quantum-applications-in-computer-aided-engineering-simulation-and-testing/
153. "Wallenberg Center for Quantum Technology". Chalmers, 2024. https://www.chalmers.se/en/centres/wacqt/
154. "How Is Using Generative AI Not Considered Theft?". Inc. 2024. https://www.inc.com/joe-procopio/how-is-using-generative-ai-not-considered-theft/91034830
155. "Google DeepMind predicts weather more accurately than leading system". The Guardian, 2024. https://www.theguardian.com/science/2024/dec/04/google-deepmind-predicts-weather-more-accurately-than-leading-system
156. "Exploring quantum computing use cases for financial services". IBM. https://www.ibm.com/thought-leadership/institute-business-value/en-us/report/exploring-quantum-financial
157. "Quantum Computing in Finance: How Banks Are Adopting Quantum Tech (Latest Stats)". PatentPC, 2025. https://patentpc.com/blog/quantum-computing-in-finance-how-banks-are-adopting-quantum-tech-latest-stats
158. "Quantum Technology Use Cases in Finance & Banking".

1. https://nypost.com/2024/04/01/self-driving-semi-trucks-have-already-hit-the-road/?utm_source=chatgpt.com

PostQuantum, 2024.
https://postquantum.com/quantum-computing/use-cases-finance-banking/

159. "Preparing financial services cybersecurity for quantum computing". EY, 2023.
https://www.ey.com/en_us/insights/strategy/financial-services-cybersecurity-for-quantum-computing

Appendix D: Glossary

Artificial Intelligence (AI): A field of computer science focused on creating systems that can perform tasks requiring human intelligence, such as learning, reasoning, and decision-making. AI is often paired with quantum computing to enhance processing capabilities for data analysis and predictive tasks.

Airbus: An aerospace company investing in quantum computing for applications such as materials science, optimizing aircraft design, and improving logistics and supply chains.

AlphaFold: An AI-based protein structure prediction tool developed by DeepMind (Google), which uses deep learning to predict the 3D structures of proteins with high accuracy. In recognition of its impact on scientific research, Demis Hassabis and John Jumper were awarded the 2024 Nobel Prize in Chemistry for their work on AlphaFold. Quantum computing may support similar biotechnological applications in the future.

Amazon Braket: A quantum computing service from Amazon Web Services that provides cloud-based access to quantum computers from companies like IonQ and Rigetti.

Atomic clock: A highly accurate clock that uses the vibrations of atoms (often cesium or rubidium) as a frequency standard, essential for precise timekeeping in GPS, telecommunications, and scientific research.

BASF: A global chemical company exploring quantum computing to advance materials science, improve chemical processes, and develop sustainable solutions in agriculture and manufacturing.

Bit: The basic unit of classical information, representing a binary state of 0 or 1. This is also known as classical bits.

Blockchain: A decentralized digital ledger technology used to securely record transactions across multiple computers. Quantum computing poses a potential threat to blockchain security because of its capability to break traditional cryptographic methods.

Bohr, Niels: A foundational physicist in quantum mechanics known for the Bohr model of the atom and contributions to understanding atomic structure and quantum theory.

Bolded: Bolded terms are highlighted in the text the first time they appear. This visual cue signals to the reader that the term is important and defined in the glossary.

Boston Dynamics: A robotics company known for advanced robots like Atlas and Spot, which demonstrate complex physical behaviors. Quantum computing may someday support the complex simulations required for advanced robotics.

Brain-machine interface (BMI): Technology that enables direct communication between the brain and external devices, with potential applications in rehabilitation and cognitive enhancement.

Classical computing: Traditional computing based on classical bits, limited by binary logic (0 and 1) and incapable of handling quantum properties like superposition and quantum entanglement.

Cloud computing: The delivery of computing services, including storage, processing power, and software, over the internet instead of relying on local servers or personal devices. Cloud computing allows users to access resources on demand, enabling scalability, cost efficiency, and remote collaboration. In quantum computing, platforms like IBM Quantum and Amazon Braket use cloud computing to provide access to quantum hardware and simulators for research and development.

Coherence: The length of time a qubit remains in a stable quantum state, crucial for maintaining quantum information during computation.

Cryptography: The practice of securing information, which is challenged by quantum computing because of its potential to break conventional encryption methods like RSA and ECC.

D-Wave Systems: A company that builds quantum annealers, a type of quantum computer specialized for optimization problems. D-Wave's systems are applied in fields like logistics, traffic flow optimization, and machine learning.

Decoherence: A phenomenon in quantum systems where qubits lose their quantum properties, such as superposition and quantum entanglement, because of interactions with their environment. Decoherence disrupts the delicate quantum states required for computations, leading to errors. Overcoming decoherence is one of the central challenges in building stable and reliable quantum computers, requiring advancements in qubit design, isolation techniques, and error correction.

Deep learning: A subset of machine learning involving neural networks with multiple layers, allowing computers to recognize patterns in huge amounts of data. Quantum computing could enhance deep learning by providing computational power for large-scale data processing.

Devs (Apple TV+): A sci-fi television series exploring quantum computing, free will, and parallel universes. The show provides a fictional look at quantum technology's potential and ethical implications.

Diamond qubits: Qubits based on nitrogen-vacancy centers in diamond, which are stable at room temperature and used in quantum sensors and potential quantum computing applications.

Digital twin: A digital replica of a physical object, system, or process used to simulate, monitor, and optimize real-world performance. Widely applied in industries such as manufacturing, urban planning, and healthcare.

Double-slit experiment: A famous physics experiment demonstrating wave-particle duality, where particles (like photons or electrons) create an interference pattern when not observed, yet behave like particles when measured. This experiment is fundamental to quantum mechanics and highlights the concept of superposition and the observer effect.

ECC (elliptic curve cryptography): A form of encryption using elliptic curves that provides security with smaller key sizes, though potentially vulnerable to quantum attacks.

Einstein, Albert: A physicist known for his theory of relativity and significant contributions to quantum mechanics, including the concept of quantum entanglement, which he famously referred to as "spooky action at a distance".

Electron: A fundamental subatomic particle with a negative electric charge. Electrons are found in atoms, orbiting the nucleus, and play a critical role in electricity, chemical reactions, and quantum mechanics. Like photons, electrons exhibit wave-particle duality, behaving as both particles and waves depending on how they are observed. Their quantum properties are essential for technologies such as transistors, electron microscopes, and quantum computing.

Error correction: Techniques used to identify and correct errors in quantum systems, essential for maintaining qubit stability and ensuring accurate calculations.

Error rates: In quantum computing, error rates refer to the frequency at which qubits produce incorrect results due to noise, instability, or interactions with the environment. High error rates are a significant challenge in quantum systems, as qubits are highly sensitive to external disturbances. Reducing error rates is essential for achieving reliable computations and is a key focus of research in areas like error correction, qubit design, and improving coherence times.

EU AI Act: A comprehensive regulation by the European Union, effective August 1, 2024, that governs the development, deployment, and use of AI technologies within the EU. It introduces a risk-based framework categorizing AI systems into risk levels, each with specific requirements to ensure safety, transparency, and protection of fundamental rights.

European Space Agency (ESA): The intergovernmental space organization focused on space exploration, satellite development, and collaboration across Europe. ESA has shown interest in quantum technologies for secure communications and space research.

Exponential growth bias: A cognitive bias where people underestimate the effects of exponential growth, often perceiving it as linear. This can lead to misunderstandings about the rapid acceleration of certain phenomena, such as technological advancements, population growth, or compound interest. In quantum computing, exponential growth bias can make it difficult to grasp how quickly qubit power scales as more qubits are added to a system.

Exponentiality: A characteristic of exponential growth where progress accelerates at an increasing rate. In technology, exponentiality refers to how advancements build on each other, leading to rapid increases in capability, often highlighted by Moore's Law and observed in quantum computing developments.

Federation: In Star Trek, an interstellar organization promoting peaceful cooperation, exploration, and ethical advancement, analogous to the collaborative ideals in advancing quantum computing.

Fujitsu: A Japanese technology company involved in developing quantum-inspired computing systems and collaborating on quantum research for fields such as materials science, logistics, and optimization.

Generative AI: A form of AI that generates new content, such as text, images, or music, based on learned patterns from large datasets. Quantum computing could improve generative AI by accelerating data processing and enhancing model training.

Goldilocks zone: The habitable zone around a star where conditions may support liquid water on a planet's surface, essential for potential life. The concept is relevant in exoplanet research and space exploration.

Google: A technology company with a significant quantum research division, Google Quantum AI, which aims to develop quantum computing capabilities. Google's Sycamore processor achieved quantum supremacy in 2019, completing a task deemed infeasible for classical computers.

Google Sycamore: Google's 54-qubit superconducting quantum processor, which achieved quantum supremacy by completing a computation that would be infeasible for classical supercomputers.

Grover's algorithm: A quantum algorithm for searching unsorted databases faster than classical algorithms, highlighting quantum speedup in search tasks.

Heisenberg, Werner: A key figure in quantum mechanics, known for the Heisenberg Uncertainty Principle, which states that certain properties of particles, such as position and momentum, cannot be precisely measured simultaneously.

High-Frequency Trading (HFT): A financial trading strategy that uses algorithms to execute large numbers of orders at extremely high speeds. Quantum computing has potential in HFT by enabling faster data analysis and decision-making.

Honeywell: A technology company known for developing trapped ion quantum computers, which are known for high accuracy and long coherence times. Honeywell's quantum division merged with Cambridge Quantum to form Quantinuum.

HQS Quantum Simulations: A German company focused on creating quantum algorithms and simulations for industrial applications, particularly in materials science and chemistry.

Hybrid quantum-classical system: A computational setup that combines quantum and classical processors, allowing each system to perform tasks suited to its strengths.

IBM Eagle: IBM's 127-qubit quantum processor, known for its improved architecture and capability to handle more complex quantum calculations, representing a step toward achieving quantum advantage.

IBM Hummingbird: A 65-qubit quantum processor developed by IBM, part of its roadmap to build increasingly powerful superconducting quantum computers.

IBM Quantum Platform: IBM's cloud-based platform that provides public access to IBM's quantum processors, allowing researchers, students, and developers to experiment with quantum circuits.

Interference: In physics, interference occurs when two or more waves overlap, resulting in a new wave pattern. This can lead to constructive interference, where waves combine to create a stronger wave, or destructive interference, where waves cancel each other out. In quantum mechanics, interference is observed in experiments like the double-slit experiment, where particles like photons or electrons produce patterns that resemble overlapping waves.

IonQ: A company specializing in ion-trap quantum computing, known for building quantum processors with long coherence times and high stability.

James Webb Space Telescope: A space observatory launched by NASA to explore deep space and gather data on the origins of the universe. Quantum computing can aid in analyzing complex astronomical data from observatories like the James Webb.

John Deere See & Spray: An agricultural technology developed by John Deere that uses AI to differentiate crops from weeds, applying herbicide only where needed. Quantum computing could further optimize such precision agriculture methods.

Large Language Model (LLM): A type of AI model trained on extensive text data to understand and generate human language, enabling applications such as chatbots, translation, and content generation.

Los Alamos National Laboratory (LANL): A U.S. research facility known for nuclear and quantum research. LANL conducts advanced studies in quantum computing, cryptography, and national security.

M-class planet: A term from Star Trek denoting planets suitable for human life, typically located within a star's habitable zone, similar to Earth-like planets in real-world exoplanet research.

Machine learning: A branch of AI that enables systems to learn and improve from data without explicit programming. Machine learning benefits from quantum computing's ability to handle complex datasets and perform high-speed calculations.

Majorana qubits: Hypothetical qubits that rely on Majorana particles, which are their own antiparticles. Majorana qubits are theorized to be highly stable and resistant to errors, making them suitable for fault-tolerant quantum computing.

Many-worlds theory: An interpretation of quantum mechanics proposed by physicist Hugh Everett III, which suggests that every quantum event results in a branching of the universe into multiple, parallel realities. In this theory, all possible outcomes of a quantum event occur, each in its own separate universe. For example, in the double-slit experiment, a photon passes through one slit in one universe and the other slit in a parallel universe. The many-worlds theory eliminates the need for wavefunction collapse and has sparked debates in science and popular culture about the nature of reality and parallel worlds.

Massachusetts Institute of Technology (MIT): A prestigious research university located in Cambridge, Massachusetts, USA. Known for its cutting-edge work in science, engineering, and technology, MIT is a leader in quantum research, advancing fields such as quantum computing, quantum information science, and quantum communication. The university hosts multiple initiatives aimed at developing quantum algorithms, improving hardware, and addressing challenges in cryptography and secure data systems.

Microsoft Azure Quantum: Microsoft's quantum cloud platform that offers access to quantum computers from various providers and a range of development tools.

Microsoft Quantum Development Kit: Microsoft's set of tools for quantum programming, featuring the Q# language for writing quantum algorithms.

Micius satellite: A Chinese satellite that demonstrated quantum communication over long distances using entangled photons, showcasing advancements in quantum encryption and secure communication.

Moore's law: The observation that classical computing power doubles roughly every two years, often referenced in discussions of exponential technological growth and limitations in classical computing.

NASA: The United States National Aeronautics and Space Administration, which explores quantum applications in space missions, data processing, and complex problem-solving for space exploration.

National Renewable Energy Laboratory (NREL): A U.S. laboratory focused on advancing sustainable energy solutions. NREL is exploring quantum computing's role in renewable energy modeling, storage, and distribution optimization.

Natural language processing (NLP): A branch of AI focused on enabling computers to understand, interpret, and generate human language. NLP powers technologies like speech recognition, machine translation, chatbots, and sentiment analysis. In the context of quantum computing, NLP could benefit from quantum algorithms that handle large datasets more efficiently, potentially improving the speed and accuracy of language-based AI applications.

Neuralink: A neurotechnology company founded by Elon Musk in 2016 focused on developing implantable brain-machine interfaces (BMIs). Neuralink aims to create devices that enable direct communication between the human brain and computers, with potential applications in treating neurological conditions and enhancing human cognition.

Neural networks: Computational models inspired by the human brain's structure, consisting of layers of interconnected nodes (neurons) that process information. Quantum computing has the potential to advance neural networks by providing more efficient ways to process complex data.

NIST (National Institute of Standards and Technology): A U.S. agency that establishes standards across various scientific fields, including quantum technologies. NIST is actively involved in developing quantum-safe encryption standards.

NISQ (noisy intermediate-scale quantum): A term describing the current era of quantum devices, which are powerful but limited by noise and error rates, making them suitable for only specific applications.

OpenAI: An AI research organization focused on developing advanced AI technologies, including language models like GPT. OpenAI's work explores ethical AI and collaborative research in AI development.

Oppenheimer, J. Robert: Theoretical physicist who led the Manhattan Project and contributed to atomic theory, with implications that spurred further developments in quantum mechanics.

Optimization: The process of finding the best solution to a problem by minimizing or maximizing a specific objective, such as cost, time, or efficiency, within given constraints. In quantum computing, optimization problems are a key application area, as quantum algorithms like QAOA (Quantum Approximate Optimization Algorithm) can evaluate multiple possibilities simultaneously, making them well-suited for tasks like supply chain management, portfolio optimization, and traffic flow analysis.

Parallelism through qubits: A unique property of quantum computing where qubits, using superposition, can represent multiple states simultaneously. This enables quantum computers to process many possibilities at once, offering a form of parallelism far beyond classical systems. For example, while a classical bit can represent only 0 or 1 at a time, a qubit can represent both 0 and 1 simultaneously, allowing quantum computers to explore multiple solutions to a problem in parallel.

Photon: The fundamental particle of light and all other forms of electromagnetic radiation. Photons are massless, travel at the speed of light, and exhibit both wave-like and particle-like behavior, a phenomenon known as wave-particle duality. They are key to understanding quantum mechanics and are used in technologies like lasers, solar cells, and quantum communication.

Photonic qubits: Qubits that use photons (particles of light) to encode information, often used in quantum communication and certain types of quantum computers because of their low noise and stability.

Planck, Max: A foundational physicist in quantum mechanics known for Planck's constant, which relates the energy of a photon to its frequency. His work laid the groundwork for quantum theory.

Post-quantum cryptography (PQC): A branch of cryptography focused on developing algorithms that are secure against attacks from quantum computers. These algorithms run on classical computers and rely on mathematical problems, such as lattice-based or multivariate polynomial cryptography, that are hard for both classical and quantum computers to solve. PQC ensures that data transmitted or stored today will remain secure even after quantum computers capable of breaking current encryption standards are developed.

Prime directive: In Star Trek, an ethical guideline preventing interference with less advanced civilizations, symbolizing the ethical considerations in quantum computing advancements, especially in areas like privacy, security, and fair access.

Qiskit: An open-source quantum computing framework developed by IBM, allowing developers to write quantum programs and simulate or run them on IBM quantum computers.

QuAIL (Quantum Artificial Intelligence Laboratory): NASA's Quantum AI Lab which collaborates with Google and others to explore quantum applications in space exploration, complex simulations, and AI. QuAIL studies how quantum computing can solve optimization problems for space missions and large datasets.

Quantinuum: A company formed from the merger of Honeywell Quantum Solutions and Cambridge Quantum, focused on developing quantum computing solutions for industries like materials science, pharmaceuticals, and cybersecurity.

Quantum-as-a-Service (QaaS): A model where quantum computing resources are provided over the cloud, enabling users to access quantum computers remotely without owning physical hardware. Providers like IBM, Amazon, and Microsoft offer QaaS.

Quantum advantage: The point at which a quantum computer performs a practical task more efficiently than a classical computer.

Quantum Approximate Optimization Algorithm (QAOA): A quantum algorithm designed to solve combinatorial optimization problems, where the goal is to find the best solution from a finite set of possibilities. QAOA combines quantum operations with classical optimization techniques to iteratively refine solutions. It is particularly well-suited for tasks like scheduling, route optimization, and portfolio management. QAOA is often used in hybrid quantum-classical systems, leveraging the strengths of both to tackle complex real-world problems efficiently.

Quantum circuit: The sequence of quantum gates and operations that act on qubits to perform a quantum computation.

Quantum crosstalk: A type of interference that occurs in quantum computers when operations on one qubit unintentionally affect nearby qubits. This can lead to errors in computations and is a significant challenge in scaling quantum systems. Reducing quantum crosstalk involves improving qubit isolation, circuit design, and control systems to minimize unintended interactions.

Quantum cryptography: A secure form of encryption based on quantum mechanics, with potential applications in secure communication and data protection.

Quantum dot qubits: Qubits formed in nanoscale semiconductor structures known as quantum dots, where the spin of electrons or electron pairs can represent quantum states. Quantum dots are explored for their potential scalability in quantum computing.

Quantum entanglement: The phenomenon where particles become interconnected and share states, even across large distances, foundational to quantum teleportation and communication.

Quantum Flagship: A €1 billion European initiative launched in 2018 to advance quantum technologies over ten years. It brings together researchers, industry, and policymakers to establish Europe as a leader in quantum fields, such as computing, simulation, communication, and sensing. The Quantum Flagship envisions a "Quantum Web" connecting quantum devices and networks across Europe.

Quantum internet: A theoretical future network based on quantum mechanics, potentially enabling secure communication channels and distributed quantum computing.

Quantum key distribution (QKD): A quantum-secure method for sharing cryptographic keys, providing high security against eavesdropping.

Quantum machine learning (QML): The application of quantum computing to machine learning algorithms, potentially improving processing speeds for large datasets.

Quantum mechanics: The branch of physics studying subatomic particles and their behaviors, foundational to quantum computing.

Quantum noise: The random interference that affects qubits, impacting the reliability of quantum computations and limiting current devices' accuracy.

Quantum sensors: Devices that use quantum properties to achieve extremely sensitive measurements in fields like navigation, healthcare, and environmental monitoring.

Quantum simulation: The use of quantum computers to model complex systems, especially useful in molecular simulations for drug discovery, materials science, and chemistry.

Quantum simulators: Software tools or specialized hardware designed to model quantum systems, allowing researchers to test and develop quantum algorithms without needing access to physical quantum computers. Quantum simulators can mimic the behavior of qubits and quantum operations, providing insights into how quantum algorithms perform under different conditions. They are widely used for experimentation, debugging, and education in quantum computing.

Quantum supremacy: The achievement of a quantum computer performing a task that is beyond the capabilities of classical computers, demonstrating a unique advantage in speed or efficiency.

Quantum teleportation: The process of transferring the quantum state of one particle to another particle at a different location without physically moving the particle itself. Quantum teleportation relies on quantum entanglement and has potential applications in secure communication and quantum networks. A notable example is China's Micius satellite, which successfully demonstrated quantum teleportation over long distances by entangling photons and transmitting quantum information from Earth to orbit, marking a major milestone in quantum communication.

Qubit: The basic unit of quantum information, capable of existing in multiple states simultaneously through superposition, which enables quantum parallelism.

Reinforcement learning: A machine learning technique where an algorithm learns by interacting with an environment, receiving rewards or penalties for its actions, and optimizing its behavior to maximize cumulative reward. It's like training a dog, where the dog learns to perform tricks by receiving treats as rewards for correct behavior.

Rigetti Computing: A quantum computing company focused on building superconducting quantum processors and providing cloud-based quantum computing services.

RSA encryption: A classical encryption method widely used in secure communications, which may be vulnerable to quantum algorithms like Shor's algorithm.

Satoshi Nakamoto: The pseudonymous individual or group that created Bitcoin and authored its white paper. Quantum computing raises concerns for blockchain and cryptocurrencies like Bitcoin because of potential vulnerabilities in cryptographic security.

Schrödinger, Erwin: A physicist known for the Schrödinger equation, which describes how quantum states evolve, and the thought experiment "Schrödinger's Cat", which illustrates the concept of superposition.

Shor's algorithm: A quantum algorithm that can factorize large numbers exponentially faster than classical algorithms, posing a threat to encryption methods like RSA.

Smart Nation Initiative (Singapore): A program by the Singaporean government to integrate digital technology into urban infrastructure, aiming to improve quality of life, economic development, and urban efficiency.

SpaceX: A private aerospace company interested in applying quantum computing to optimize mission logistics, resource management, and sustainable space exploration.

Spin qubits: Qubits that store information using the spin state of electrons or nuclei, typically within semiconductor materials. Spin qubits are promising for their small size and potential scalability in solid-state quantum computers.

Spooky action at a distance: A phrase coined by Albert Einstein to describe quantum entanglement, where two particles become linked in such a way that the state of one instantly influences the other, regardless of distance.

Starfleet academy: In Star Trek, an institution where future explorers are trained, symbolizing the importance of education and skill development for future quantum computing specialists.

Superconducting qubits: A type of qubit used in many quantum computers (including those by IBM and Google) based on superconducting circuits that exhibit quantum properties at very low temperatures.

Superposition: A quantum state where a qubit can exist as both 0 and 1 simultaneously, providing the foundation for quantum parallelism.

Supervised learning: A machine learning technique where an algorithm learns from labeled data, making predictions or decisions based on the patterns it identifies. It's like a student learning from a teacher, with the labeled data serving as the textbook and the correct answers.

Topological qubit: A theoretical type of qubit that encodes information in topological states, potentially offering greater resistance to errors and supporting fault-tolerant quantum computing.

Transistor: A semiconductor device that acts as a switch or amplifier in electronics, foundational to classical computing and technology miniaturization.

Trapped ion: A technology for building quantum computers using ions held in place by electromagnetic fields, known for stability and long coherence times.

Trapped ion qubits: Qubits that use ions trapped and manipulated with electromagnetic fields. Known for their long coherence times and accuracy, trapped ion qubits are used by companies such as IonQ and Honeywell.

Traveling Salesman Problem (TSP): A classic optimization problem that seeks the shortest possible route connecting a list of cities and returning to the starting point. Quantum computing's ability to handle complex optimizations may offer new solutions to TSP and similar logistical problems.

Uncertainty principle: A key concept in quantum mechanics, introduced by Werner Heisenberg, stating that it is impossible to precisely know both the position and velocity of a particle at the same time. This limitation is not because of flaws in measurement but is a fundamental property of quantum systems. The uncertainty principle highlights how observation itself can influence a particle's behavior, reshaping our understanding of measurement and reality at the quantum scale.

Unsupervised learning: A machine learning technique where an algorithm explores unlabeled data to discover hidden patterns, structures, or groupings. It's like a detective trying to solve a case without any prior clues, relying solely on the evidence to uncover the truth.

Urban Twin (IBM): IBM's **digital twin** concept applied to cities, creating a digital representation of urban environments to help simulate, monitor, and optimize city systems for improved planning and sustainability.

Volkswagen's Quantum Lab: Volkswagen's research initiative focused on applying quantum computing to solve mobility challenges, including traffic optimization and electric vehicle battery development.

Wallenberg Centre for Quantum Technology (WACQT): A Swedish national research initiative based at Chalmers University of Technology, focused on advancing quantum technology. Supported by a 12-year funding program of approximately $100 million, WACQT aims to build a 100-qubit quantum computer using superconducting circuits. The center also conducts research in quantum communication, quantum sensing, and quantum simulation, collaborating with other Swedish universities and international partners to drive innovation. WACQT's mission is to position Sweden as a leader in the global quantum technology landscape.

Wave-particle duality: A fundamental concept in quantum mechanics that shows particles, such as photons and electrons, can exhibit both wave-like and particle-like behavior depending on how they are observed. For example, in the double-slit experiment, particles create an interference pattern like waves when unobserved but act like individual particles when measured. This discovery challenged classical physics and became a cornerstone of quantum theory.

Xanadu: A Canadian company established in 2016, specializing in photonic quantum computing and quantum machine learning software. Xanadu develops quantum computers that utilize light (photons) for processing, aiming to make quantum computing more accessible and scalable. They also offer a cloud-based platform for users to access their quantum hardware.

Xiong'an New Area: A *smart city* project in China designed to use advanced technologies, including AI and potentially quantum computing, for efficient urban management and sustainable growth.

Acknowledgments

Thank you to everyone who helped, inspired, or encouraged me while I wrote this book. A special thanks to Nathalie. And thank you to you, the reader, for giving it your time.

About the Author

Tommy Wassgren has built a career at the intersection of technology and leadership, with many years of experience in coding, AI, and tech innovation. Through various roles, he has developed a strong understanding of both the technical and human dimensions of the field. Known for his expertise in cultivating creativity and a collaborative culture, Tommy is dedicated to advancing teams and ideas with purpose.

Driven by the excitement of quantum technology's potential, Tommy brings a unique perspective as a tech expert and enthusiast. In *Don't Open the Box*, he shares this sense of wonder with readers, presenting complex concepts in an accessible, engaging guide to the future of computing.

Read more at https://www.linkedin.com/in/wassgren/.